do it **NOW** *do it* **FAST** *do it* **RIGHT**®

Bathroom

Makeovers

do it **NOW** *do it* **FAST** *do it* **RIGHT**®

Bathroom

Makeovers

The Taunton Press

The Taunton Press, Inc., 63 South Main Street, PO Box 5506, Newtown, CT 06470-5506

e-mail: tp@taunton.com

PRODUCED BY HOME & GARDEN EDITORIAL SERVICES

PROJECT MANAGER: Joe Provey

WRITER: Roy Barnhart

SERIES DESIGN: Lori Wendin

LAYOUT: Jill Schoff

ILLUSTRATOR: Charles Lockhart

PHOTOGRAPHER: Carl Weese

COVER PHOTOGRAPHERS: All cover photographs by Carl Weese, except front
cover main photo © Randy O'Rourke; back cover bottom left and third from
left © Roger Turk/Northlight Photography, Inc., and bottom second from right
© Brian Vanden Brink, photographer

Taunton's Do It Now/Do It Fast/Do It Right® is a trademark of
The Taunton Press, Inc., registered in the U.S. Patent and Trademark Office.

LIBRARY OF CONGRESS CATALOGING-IN-PUBLICATION DATA

Bathroom makeovers.

    p. cm. -- (Do it now/do it fast/do it right)

 ISBN 1-56158-727-3

 1. Bathrooms----Remodeling--Amateurs' manuals. I. Taunton Press. II. Series.

 TT4816.3.B37B375 2005

 643'.52--dc22

                 2004028027

Printed in the United States of America

10 9 8 7 6 5 4 3 2 1

The following manufacturers/names appearing in *Bathroom Makeovers* are trademarks: EZ Toggler®; Hardibacker®;
Speed® Square; Teflon®; Toggler® Alligator®; Toggler® Snaptoggle®.

Acknowledgments

Thanks to Dalton Ghetti, Christian and Sandy Hartgens, Patrick Hughes, Valerie Jouan, Corinna Provey, Joe Provey Jr., Dagan Reinhardt, Dylan Reinhardt, Mikaelle Rosw, Frank Saum, and Caline Wells—all of whom helped to make this book possible.

We'd also want to thank the following corporations for supplying expertise, products, and photography: American Standard Companies, American Olean Co., Broan-NuTone LLC, Kohler Company, LTL Home Products, Masco Corporation (Liberty Hardware), Porter Cable Corporation, Quality Doors, Stone House Building Products (Cermaxx), Tech Lighting LLC, Thomas Lighting, Mechanical Plastics Corp., Skil Tools, and The Swan Corporation.

Contents

Bathroom PROJECTS

Prep Projects **16**

Before undergoing **BATHROOM UPGRADES,** ready the walls and ceilings with these tips and techniques

Painted Vanity Cabinet **24**

Give your bathroom cabinets a new identity with **PAINT** & **HARDWARE**

Helpful Hang-Ups **36**

Put bathroom walls to work by installing **BARS, HOOKS** & **PEGS**

Painted Wainscot Walls **44**

Warm up your bathroom with easy-to-install **WAINSCOT PANELS**

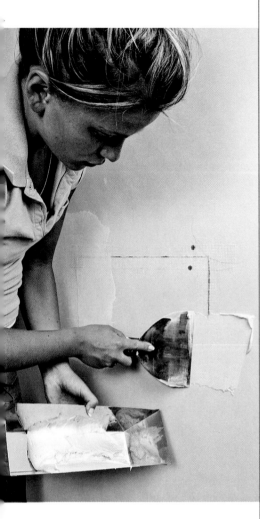

How to Use This Book

I F YOU'RE INTERESTED IN HOME IMPROVEMENTS that add value and convenience while also enabling you to express your own sense of style, you've come to the right place. **Do It Now/Do It Fast/Do It Right** books are created with an attitude that says "Let's get started!" and an ideal mix of home-improvement inspiration and how-to information. Do It Now books don't skip important steps or force you to guess at what needs to be done to take a project from start to finish.

You'll find that this book has a friendly, easy-to-use format. (See the sample pages shown here.) You'll begin each project knowing exactly what tools and gear you'll need, and what materials to buy at your home center or building-supply outlet. You can get started confidently because every step is illustrated and explained. Along the way, you'll discover plenty of expert advice packed into the margins. For ideas on how to personalize your project, check out the design options pages that follow the step-by-step instructions.

WORK TOGETHER

If you like company when you go to the movies or clean up the kitchen, you'll probably feel the same way about tackling home-improvement projects. The work will go faster, and you'll have a partner to share in the adventure. You'll

Get the TOOLS & GEAR you need. You'll also find out what features and details are important.

WHAT CAN GO WRONG explains how to avoid common mistakes.

SAFETY FIRST helps you keep you and your project free of accidents and hazards.

DO IT RIGHT tells you what it takes to get top-notch results.

WHAT TO BUY helps you put together your project shopping list, so you get all the materials you need.

COOL TOOL puts you in touch with tools that make the job easier.

see that some projects really call for another set of hands to steady a ladder or keep the project going smoothly. Read through the project you'd like to tackle, and note where you're most likely to need help.

PLANNING AND PRACTICE PAY OFF

Most of the projects in this book can easily be completed in a weekend. But the job can take longer if you don't pay attention to planning and project-preparation requirements. Check out the conditions in the area where you'll be working in case repairs are required before you can begin your project. In the GET SET chapter (beginning on the next page), you'll find useful information on getting organized and on many of the tools, fasteners, and glue used in storage projects.

Your skill and confidence will improve with every project you complete. But if you're trying a technique for the first time, it's wise to rehearse before you "go live." This means ordering a little extra in the way of supplies and materials, and finding a location where you can practice your technique.

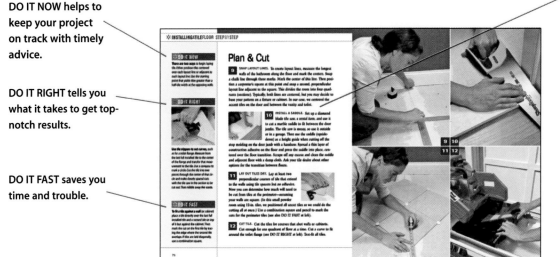

DESIGN OPTIONS Personalize your project with dimensions, finishes, and details that suit your space and your sense of style.

DO IT NOW helps to keep your project on track with timely advice.

DO IT RIGHT tells you what it takes to get top-notch results.

DO IT FAST saves you time and trouble.

STEP BY STEP Get started, keep going, and finish the job. Every step is illustrated and explained.

Get Set

Get your project off to the right start with some
TOOL, SKILL & SAFETY basics

WHEN MAKING IMPROVEMENTS in a bathroom, you may find yourself needing skills from a half-dozen building trades. Don't let that intimidate you, even if you are tackling your first do-it-yourself home improvement project. You can get started with a modest investment in tools, and the skills can easily be learned as you go. Just be sure to take full advantage of all resources—read product instructions and tool manuals, call manufacturers' toll-free help lines, and consult knowledgeable salespeople where you buy your supplies. Now, let's take a look at some of the skills, tools, and materials you'll be using for the projects in this book.

❖ COOL TOOL

An electrician's cabinet screwdriver allows you to twist a loop in the end of a wire and tighten the terminal screw with a single tool.

❖ LINGO

A pigtail allows you to connect two wires to a screw terminal. Make one by twisting one end of a short length of wire together with two wires. Secure the twisted end under a wire nut, and then connect the other end of the length of wire (the pigtail) to the screw terminal. Never connect two wires directly to a screw terminal.

Electrical Wiring Done Right

Bathroom makeovers often involve simple electrical projects. A novice can handle these easily, as long as safety guidelines are observed and the proper tools and techniques are used.

WIRING SAFETY

BE DOUBLY SAFE. The first rule is to always shut off the power for the circuit in question at the main circuit panel. To do so, you will either flick a circuit breaker to the "OFF" position or, in some older homes, unscrew a fuse.

The wires in an outlet box may be powered by more than one circuit. For that reason always use a neon circuit tester to determine if power has been cut off to all wires. Touch one probe to each black or red (hot) conductor, or to the brass screw terminal it's connected to on the outlet. Connect the other probe to any white (neutral) conductor, to its silver screw terminal, or to the bare (ground) wire. If the probe won't fit under a wire nut, temporarily twist it off to perform your test. If the circuit tester glows it means the circuit is live and you've got another breaker or fuse to disconnect.

MAKE SENSE OF WIRING. Typical wiring projects involve only two wires. The "hot" wire is either black or red; the "neutral" wire is white. A bare or green "ground" wire is a safety feature that only carries current if there is a problem with the wiring. If your connection has more than two wires, wrap a bit of masking tape around each wire as you disconnect it. Write what the wire should be reconnected to on the tape. Alternately, as you remove a wire from an old fixture, connect it to the same place on the new fixture.

WIRING SKILLS

STRIP WIRES PROPERLY. Use a wire stripper to remove the insulation from the wire ends. The numbers

next to the cutters indicate the wire gauge—14 and 12 are the ones you'll use most. Cut off only as much as will fit under a screw head on a fixture or inside a wire nut. No bare wire should extend past the screw or nut or you may create a short-circuit hazard.

JOINING WIRES.
When joining two or more solid (non-stranded) wires under a wire nut, you must first twist the wires together.

Just cross and grasp the wires as shown with long-nose pliers, and then twist the ends clockwise with lineman's pliers. When joining a stranded wire, such as one from a fixture, to a solid wire (or to two solid wires already twisted together), just twist the stranded one clockwise around the solid wire(s) with your fingers, then tightly screw on a wire nut.

CONNECTING TO A SWITCH OR RECEPTACLE. Use long-nose pliers to twist an open loop at the end of a wire and make sure it fits clockwise around the terminal screw so that

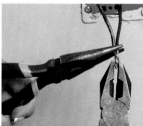

when the screw is tightened it closes, not opens, the loop. Don't allow the uninsulated part of a wire to extend past a screw head. Also, the electrical code prohibits connecting more than one wire under a screw—so create a pigtail if needed (see LINGO at left).

An electrician's tool pouch usually includes a utility knife, screwdrivers, lineman's pliers, wire strippers, and long-nose pliers. Whenever possible choose tools with insulated handles as an extra precaution against getting shocked. They have a solid grip and are more comfortable as well.

Plumbing Savvy

Save money and time by tackling the simple plumbing projects that you're likely to encounter in a bathroom makeover—and put the money into a new faucet or fixture. Just remember that there are pipes inside the walls. This means that when you are cutting, drilling, nailing, or screwing into a wall, be sure not to puncture any pipes!

Examples of a fixture shutoff (above) and a main shutoff (below).

KNOW THE SYSTEM

WATER LINES. Hot and cold water lines need to be shut off before removing or replacing a fixture. Sinks and toilets usually have valves under or next to them for easy shut off. When working on the tub or shower, you may have to find a valve (behind an access panel or in the basement) that shuts off water to the whole bathroom. If you can't shut off water at the valve, shut off all water to the house at the main valve where the water line comes in from the street or well. Remember, there will still be water in the lines that will drain when a connection is opened, so have a bucket or towel handy.

DRAIN LINES. Drain lines carry wastewater from a fixture to a sewer or septic system. To prevent sewer gasses from entering the house, each fixture drain has a U-shaped bend in the pipe called a trap. As long as the trap is filled with water, gasses cannot enter the home. If you must remove a trap, tightly stuff the opening with a rag. The trap for a toilet is built into the toilet bowl, so if you remove the toilet, stuff the opening with a rag.

TUB/SHOWER CONNECTIONS

Shower arm to drop fitting & showerhead to shower arm

Threaded tub spout/nipple

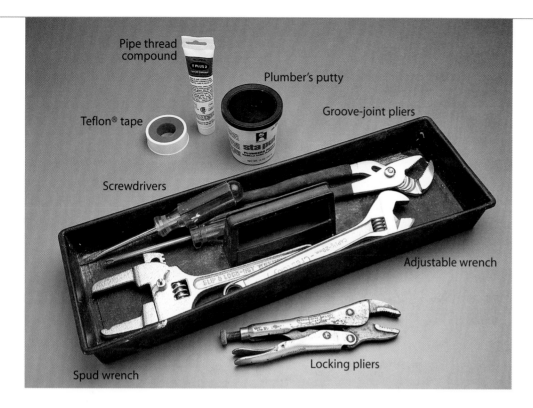

Pipe thread compound

Plumber's putty

Teflon® tape

Groove-joint pliers

Screwdrivers

Adjustable wrench

Spud wrench

Locking pliers

The tools shown here are relatively inexpensive and will last a lifetime.

IT'S ALL ABOUT CONNECTIONS

Whatever the material or type of connection, tighten until snug and then only a little more, as needed to stop a leak. Most of the connections you will encounter (see photos below) require a wrench or groove-joint pliers; a couple may only require hand-tightening; and some require a sealant for a leak-proof seal, as indicated in the photos below and below left.

WATER LINE CONNECTIONS

Faucet to sink/counter

Faucets to spout

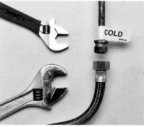
Supply tube to faucet

Shutoff to supply tube

DRAIN LINE CONNECTIONS

Drain to sink/counter

Drain/stopper/tailpiece

Stopper/lift rod

Trap assembly

Carpentry Kit

USING TOOLS SAFELY

Using power tools, such as a circular saw or jigsaw, is safe if you read and follow the tool's instruction manual (which can often be downloaded from the manufacturer's Web site). The instructions will describe how to properly support and clamp a workpiece,

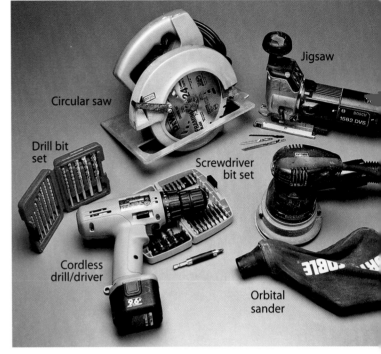

Circular saw

Jigsaw

Drill bit set

Screwdriver bit set

Cordless drill/driver

Orbital sander

how to hold and guide the tool, safety features, accessories, and much more. Whenever you are cutting, hammering, or drilling, be sure to wear eye protection. Use earplugs, dust masks, and kneepads, as needed.

NEW AGE FASTENING

While the hammer still has its place, you'll find that cordless drill/drivers and coarse-threaded "drywall" screws will be used for most fastening jobs in our projects. Buy at least a ½-in. 12-volt drill/driver with an extra battery so you're less likely to run out of juice. You may want to purchase a separate accessory kit and also a drill set for both regular and masonry bits. Buy other accessories, such as hole saws, as you need them.

ATTACHING TO WALLS. If you are going to attach something to a wall, it helps to know what the wall is made of and what's behind it. In most homes today, walls are framed with wood studs (either 2x4s or 2x6s) and covered with gypsum wallboard, commonly referred to as drywall. Drywall won't hold a screw like wood, so hollow-wall anchors must be

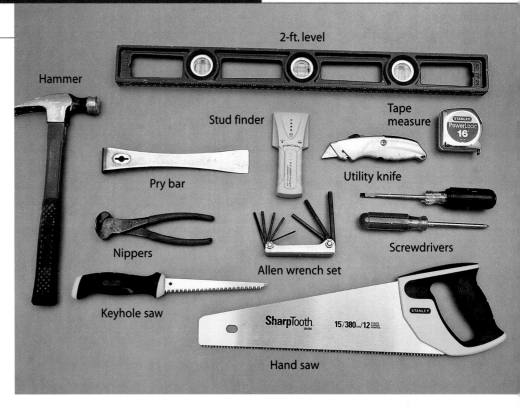

Hammer

2-ft. level

Stud finder

Tape measure

Pry bar

Utility knife

Nippers

Allen wrench set

Screwdrivers

Keyhole saw

SharpTooth 15/380mm/12

Hand saw

used when your fastener doesn't happen to fall on a stud. Anchors are rated according to the weight they can support or as light-, medium-, or heavy-duty. The strongest are those that lock onto the back side of the board (see WALL ANCHORS, below).

DEALING WITH PLASTER. Older homes have plaster walls and ceilings. Plaster is applied over screen-like metal lath, strips of thin wood called wood lath, or gypsum panels. Plaster won't accept screw- or nail-in anchors, so you must drill a pilot hole and use an anchor suitable for plaster. You will ruin a regular steel drill bit drilling plaster. Use a masonry bit instead (see DO IT RIGHT at left). The same is true when drilling into tile.

FINDING THE STUDS. It is preferable, and sometimes essential, to attach things to solid wood, such as to a stud or to wood blocking installed between two studs, rather than to hollow wall surfaces. Wall studs are typically placed every 16 in., so if you can locate one you can usually find others by measuring from the first (see DO IT FAST at left). Try one of the following approaches:

• An electrical receptacle will be attached to a stud. Tap the wall to either side of the receptacle and listen for a hollow or solid sound. The latter would indicate a stud. If you're not sure, remove the cover plate and look.

• Shine a bright light across the wall (or baseboard trim) at a low angle, and look for imperfections that indicate fastener locations.

• If an area will be covered by trim or a cabinet, drive a 6d finishing nail about 1 in. into the wall every inch or so until you hit a stud.

• Use an electronic sensor called a stud finder. Move it across the wall slowly, and it will light or beep as it passes over framing.

WALL ANCHORS

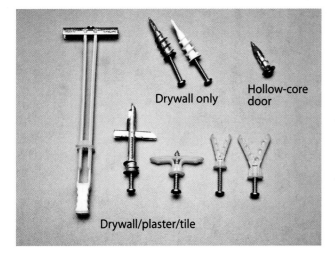

Drywall only

Hollow-core door

Drywall/plaster/tile

◆ DO IT NOW

You can fix a squeaky floor with screws, but if your floor doesn't feel solid underfoot, consult a structural engineer or reputable contractor to see what should be done to strengthen it before you lay tile.

▶ DO IT RIGHT

A straightedge is a handy tool for many projects. When tiling, lay it across the top and against the edges of set tiles to see if they are flat and in line. Make adjustments before moving on to the next section.

Tiling Basics

THE RIGHT START

A tile floor requires a solid foundation that consists of sturdy wood framing (joists), and subflooring and underlayment with a combined thickness of 1 in. To silence squeaks, drive 2-in. coarse-threaded screws through the underlayment and

into the joists. An optimal tile floor system includes a sandwich of backer board, "thin-set" adhesive (to bond the backer board to the floor and the tile to the backer board), tiles, grout to fill the joints, and sealer.

BUYING AND MIXING ADHESIVE

The most common and recommended adhesive used on tile floors is a cement-like material called thin-set. Buy one with powdered acrylic additive incorporated into the mix to make mixing foolproof. Determine the approximate quantity needed for the area to be covered and fill a bucket with about three-quarters of the water specified. Then add the powder and mix. Add additional water until the mix is just stiff enough to hold a peak. Then allow the mix to rest (called slake) for about 10 minutes and mix again. If more water is required, add it and let it rest again before mixing and using it. Follow the same procedure when mixing grout.

TILER'S TOOL KIT

Preparing for and installing tile requires a few specialized tools.

BACKERBOARD BASICS. To "cut" backerboard, you'll need a carbide scoring tool. Score the surface of the backerboard and then break it along the scored line. A drill/driver, corded or cordless, is ideal for securing backerboard to the subfloor with screws. Or simply use a hammer to drive in galvanized roofing nails.

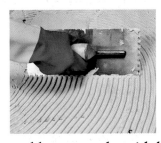

MIXING AND SPREADING. The best tool for mixing small quantities of adhesive is a margin trowel. If you own a heavy-duty drill, buy a mixing paddle for faster and better results with large batches. You'll need a notched trowel to evenly spread adhesive. Use the straight edge of a notched trowel to spread adhesive over a 3-ft.- or 4-ft.-square area. Then use the notched edge, held at a 45-degree angle, to comb the adhesive and to ensure an even distribution.

TILE CUTTING. Two tools will handle your tile-cutting chores. Use a rented tile saw (see COOL TOOL, p. 72) for making straight cuts. Use tile nippers to nibble away bits of tile at a time to make curved cuts.

GROUTING TOOLS. Work grout into the joints with a grout trowel (also called a rubber float), working back and forth diagonally. Then strike off the excess with the trowel held nearly perpendicular to the surface. Use a grout sponge to clean the grout off the surface before it dries.

Bucket

Sealer

Sponge

Grout mix

Grout trowel

You'll be amazed by how much paint you can squeeze out of a roller cover using the curved face of this 5-in-1 painter's tool. The tool is also a brush comb and scraper.

A hawk (top) has four long edges, a large surface, and a comfortable handle, making it superior to less expensive mud pans (right) for holding joint compound.

Paint & Drywall Primer

PRIMER & PAINT

You won't save much money by applying low-quality paint to the walls and ceilings of your bathroom, so buy brand names you trust that offer a warranty. Choose a 100% acrylic-based paint with mildewcide added. Because semi-gloss and satin finishes stand up better to washing and resist mildew more than a flat finish, they are

Edging pad

Roller cover

Disposable liner

Paint tray

Roller frame

Brush/roller spinner

Angled brushes

Painter's tool

Canvas drop cloth

Putty knife

better choices for a full bath. When your repairs include new drywall, apply a primer/sealer before applying the topcoat.

BUY BETTER TOOLS

As a novice or occasional painter, take advantage of the improved quality and ease of use that comes with quality tools. Cheap brushes will leave fibers in your finish.

Clean brushes well using a brush comb (far left) and paint spinner (left). Store them carefully in their original wrappers, and they will last for dozens of projects.

SELECT THE RIGHT FIBER BRUSH AND ROLLER. Brushes and rollers with natural fibers, such as boar's hair or lamb's wool, are for oil- or alkyd-based finishes. They will swell and are eventually ruined when used with latex paints. Brushes with angled tips are generally considered the most versatile for painting trim.

LOOK FOR STRONG ROLLER FRAMES. They will yield more even results than flimsy frames. "Best" quality roller covers are less likely to shed fuzz on the walls than cheap roller covers. Use short nap covers (¼ in. to ½ in. long) for smooth surfaces like drywall.

DRYWALL CUTTING TOOLS. A good-quality utility knife is essential when making drywall patches. Use it to cut through the paper facing prior to snapping the board and to cut through the paper backing afterwards. A metal straightedge or a carpenter's square will help guide your face cuts. The utility knife can also be used to make a nice square cutout around the damaged section of a wall. Make repeated passes with the knife. A pointed wallboard saw can also be used for this task. When using a saw, cut a small exploratory hole so you can check for pipe and wires first.

COMPOUND AND TAPE. Finish repairs with a minimum of three coats of premixed joint compound, available in 1- and 5-gallon containers, and fiberglass mesh or perforated paper tape over the seams. Lightweight compound dries faster but does not dry as hard as regular premixed compound. Fiberglass tape is somewhat easier for a novice to use.

APPLYING COMPOUND. A 5-in.- or 6-in.-wide taping knife is the right tool for spreading the first two coats of compound over a joint. Use a wider (10-in.) finishing knife for spreading the last coat. Use a hawk (a flat aluminum surface with a handle under it) or a mud pan to hold the compound (called mud in the trade) as you work. These tools have sharp edges upon which you can scrape your knife clean after each pass.

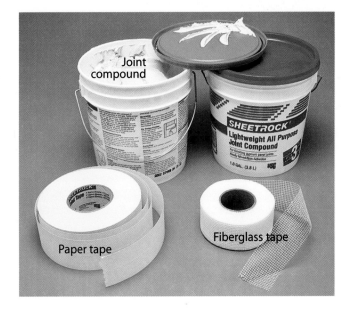

Prep Projects

Before undergoing BATHROOM UPGRADES, ready the walls and ceilings with these tips and techniques

MOLD, MILDEW, AND PAINT FAILURES TOP THE LIST of common bathroom maintenance problems. To make matters worse, they have a tendency to recur if you don't fix the underlying causes. Here you'll find advice for the best solutions, proper ventilation, and the right paint. As these improvements typically involve drywall patching and repair, you'll find a primer on that basic skill, too. Remember, it's a good rule to save your final coats of paint for the end, especially if you're planning to tackle other projects in this book. It's just too easy to mar a freshly painted wall while hefting a fixture or cabinet into place.

INSTALL A FAN   PATCH DRYWALL   ADD A TIMER   PAINT TRIM

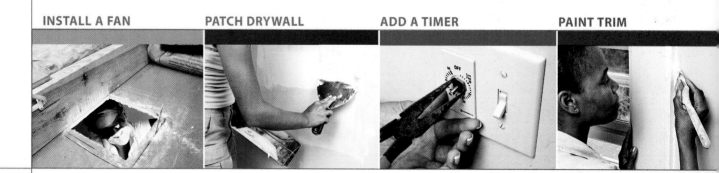

Replace a Fan

1 **REMOVE THE HOUSING.** Once the power has been shut off, remove the trim, light bulb, and reflector (if any). From the attic, push back the insulation, disconnect the duct to the fan, and loosen the electrical cable clamp. Then loosen or remove the fasteners that secure the housing to the ceiling joists and lift it off. If you don't have access from above, stand under the fan and cut out a piece of drywall from between the joists on either side of the vent and remove the fan housing from below. You'll be able to patch the ceiling later.

2 **DISCONNECT THE WIRING.** Check to be sure the electricity has been turned off (see GET SET, p. 6). Then unscrew and remove the wiring box cover and disconnect all wires.

3 **INSTALL THE ASSEMBLED UNIT.** From the attic, trace the new fan/light housing onto the ceiling and drive nails through the ceiling to mark the corners. From below, mark the cutout by connecting the screws with a pencil line. Cut an opening slightly larger than  the line using a wallboard saw (also called a jab saw). Be sure to wear eye protection and a dust mask. From above, hold the housing bottom flush to the ceiling, mark screw locations, and drive the screws in halfway. Hang the housing over the screw heads, then drive them tight. Attach the electrical cable, reconnect the duct, and reposition the insulation. Keep insulation 3 in. away from the fixture unless it is rated type IC.

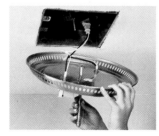

4 **COMPLETE THE WIRING.** Working from below, make final wiring and grounding connections (inset photo) and install the trim as directed by the manufacturer. To ensure adequate venting automatically, replace a standard switch with a more convenient timer following the manufacturer's instructions.

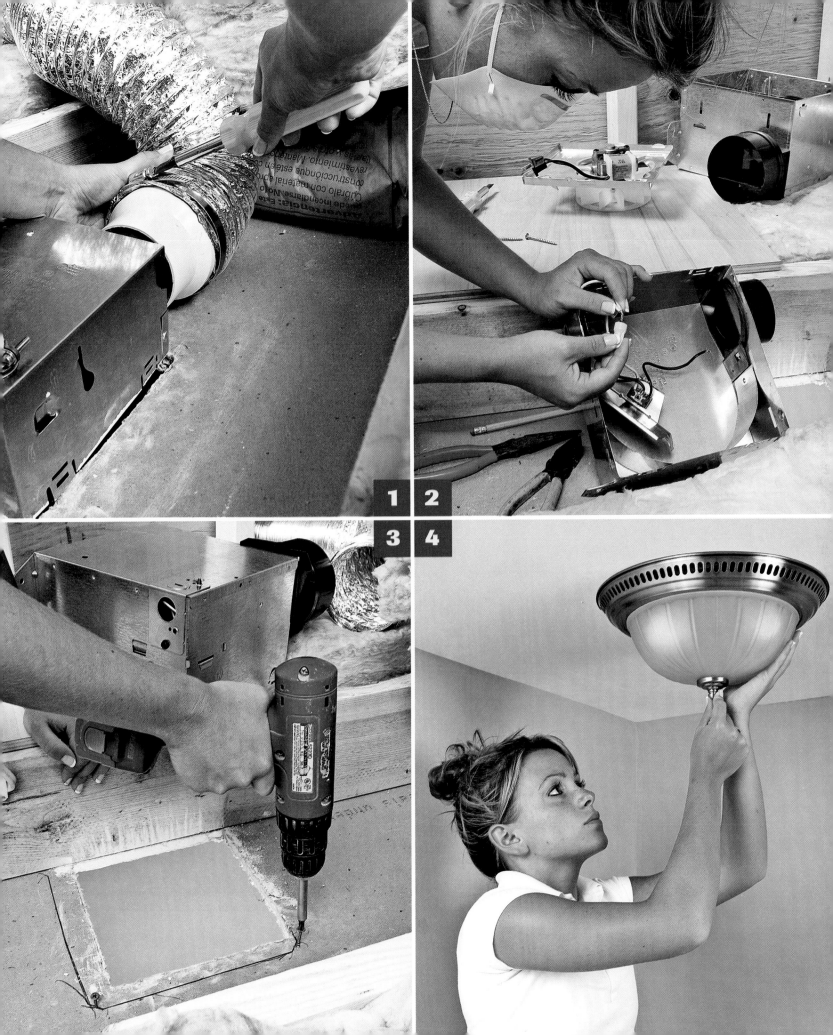

1

2

3

4

⏵ DO IT RIGHT

To guarantee a perfect fit, cut the patch first and trace it onto the wall, before cutting away the damaged area with a wallboard saw.

⦿ WHAT'S DIFFERENT?

Premixed lightweight joint compound dries faster than regular premixed compound but does not produce as hard a surface. Consequently, it requires delicate sanding—try 220-grit sandpaper or a spackle sponge.

✚ WHAT CAN GO WRONG

Avoid sanding into the paper facing, as it will become fuzzy and hard to paint well later.

Patch Drywall

1 **MAKE THE PATCH.** Measure and mark a a new piece of drywall large enough to cover the damaged area. To cut the patch, score one face of the drywall with a utility knife using a framing square as a guide. Snap the panel over the edge of a worktable so that it breaks on the scored line, and cut the paper backing on the fold. Cut out the damaged area with a wallboard saw.

2 **INSTALL THE PATCH.** Cut two nailers from scrap lumber, such as 1x4 pine, so they are about 6 in. longer than the opening in the drywall. Insert, center, and attach the nailers as shown, with a 1¼-in. drywall screw at each end. Then secure the patch to the nailers with a screw at each corner.

3 **TAPE AND MUD.** Apply pieces of self-adhering, fiberglass mesh tape over the joints, smoothing them with a taping knife; cut off the excess with a utility knife (inset photo). Working from joint compound scooped into a mud pan, use a taping knife to apply and then smooth the compound over the joints. Scrape the compound off the knife on the edge of the mud pan after each smoothing pass. Thinly cover the tape and feather the edges into the drywall. Allow the compound to dry, typically one day (it turns bright white when it's dry).

4 **APPLY MORE COATS.** Sand between coats to remove bumps if necessary and brush off sanding dust. Apply a second coat of mud, extending it past the edges of the previous coat. Let it dry and apply a third coat. If available, use a wider knife for the third coat. After the third coat, use a rubber sanding block and 120-grit sandpaper to smooth the repair. Sand only until you can no longer see or feel any ridges at the outer edges. Vacuum off dust and apply your paint primer.

✳ **DO** IT FAST

An edging pad works twice as fast as a brush for cutting in. Its rollers ride on the perpendicular surface—in this case the ceiling—so be sure to keep the rollers paint-free.

▶ **DO** IT RIGHT

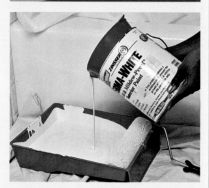

Unless you've never had a problem with mold or mildew, use only mildew-resistant paint (paint with a mildewcide added) in a full bathroom. It can be custom tinted by your dealer.

Paint a Bathroom

1 **PREPARE THE ROOM.** Don't be lazy! Remove everything you can from the room and walls (towel bars, shower curtain rods, switch plates, etc.). Remove the door and door and window hardware. If you have mold, mix a solution of 1 part laundry bleach to 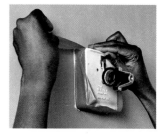 3 parts water and apply it to the walls and ceiling with a sprayer or sponge. Wait 15 minutes and repeat as necessary until stains are gone. Wipe surfaces with a neutralizing solution of 1 part vinegar to 2 parts water. Use masking tape and drop cloths to protect surfaces and fixtures.

2 **SAND AND CAULK.** Patch any holes or nail pops with lightweight spackling compound, and sand trim to "degloss" it and to correct imperfections in the finish. Apply caulk with a tube or gun to fill cracks, such as between trim and the walls or floor, or along a counter backsplash and the wall. Be sure to remove the old caulk first.

3 **PAINT TRIM.** Prime any bare wood spots. Then apply a topcoat with a 2-in. angled sash brush. It's best to work from the inside out, painting detailed areas first (window muntins, edges of door panels) and larger, flat surfaces (door and window casings) last. Allow trim paint to extend about ⅛ in. onto wall surfaces and windowpanes.

4 **PAINT CEILING AND WALLS.** Apply a band of paint along the edges of the ceiling (called cutting in) with a brush or pad, overlapping the wall slightly. Lay down a "W" pattern with your roller and then roll it out to cover a 3-ft. by 3-ft. area before moving on to the next area. Once the ceiling is painted, move on to the walls. Cut in at the top of each wall (inset photo) and at baseboards, corners, and other edges. Use a fully loaded roller to cover the walls in overlapping 1-ft. by 8-ft. sections. Reroll each section in one direction to even out the paint.

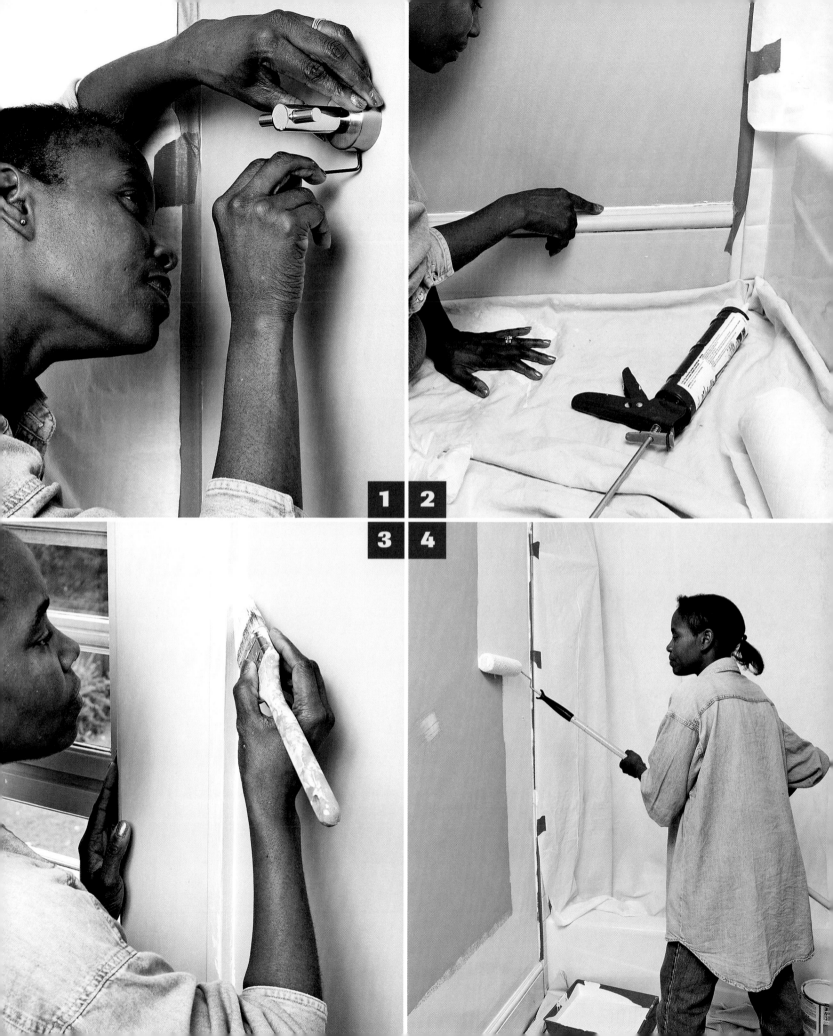

1

2

3

4

Painted Vanity Cabinet

Give your bathroom cabinets a new identity with **PAINT & HARDWARE**

I F YOU'VE GOT A DARK AND DINGY VANITY CABINET in your bathroom, a little bit of paint, some new hardware, and a touch of imagination can transform it in a weekend. The total cost, even if you don't own a brush, will be less than $50. There's no need to remove the cabinet from the room either—the work can be done in place without making a big mess. We offer three facelift options: a bright contemporary look, antiqued, and sponged. The step-by-step pages will show you how to do each of the decorative treatments.

| REMOVE HARDWARE | PREP THE SURFACE | APPLY PAINT | ANTIQUE OR SPONGE |

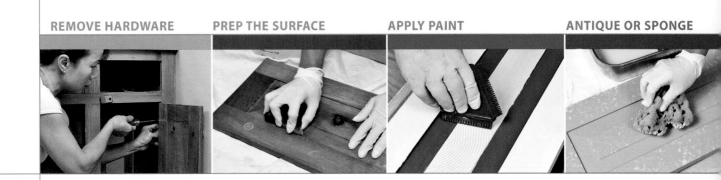

Tools & Gear

Aside from a screwdriver and sander, all you'll need are some basic paint supplies. If you're replacing the old hardware, you may also need a drill/driver to bore new hardware holes.

SCREWDRIVERS. Two sizes for Phillips and flat-head screws will normally do the trick.

CANVAS DROP CLOTH. Paper or plastic under the canvas is advisable. Canvas alone will catch drips, but not prevent seep-through from a spill.

COMBINATION SQUARE. If you need to measure for new hardware, this tool will come in handy.

PAINT BRUSHES. A 1-in. and 2-in. professional-quality sash brush should be all that you need.

PAINT TRAY. Buy one that accepts a plastic liner. It will save lots of clean-up time, not to mention lots of mess.

PAINTER'S COMB. Available at home centers and paint stores, this rubber tool allows you to remove some of a glaze topcoat to form stripes of varying widths.

SEA SPONGE. This type of sponge gives the best results and is widely available at home centers.

UTILITY KNIFE. This comes in handy for a number of things, plus you'll need it to cut the sponge if you want to try a sponging treatment.

SANDER. A random-orbit sander will speed jobs with large flat areas.

COOL TOOL

Sanding dust is a problem when you're working within the home. The best tool for minimizing dust is a shop vacuum that has an electrical outlet built into the vacuum housing. Plug your random-orbit sander into it, turn on the sander, and the vacuum activates. A hose from the vacuum connects directly to the sander (which can also be used with a less-effective dust collection bag).

What to Buy

1| SANDING SPONGES AND SANDPAPER. Medium-grit sanding sponges, which can be used damp, do the job and keep dust to a minimum. Work with a bucket of water nearby so you can rinse the sponge often. For the antiquing effect, however, use 100-grit sandpaper.

2| LIQUID SANDER. Provides a quick and sure way to ensure a good bond between paint and a previously varnished surface (see DO IT RIGHT, p. 28). It is noxious though, so only use it if you can provide ventilation with a window and fan.

3| PAINTER'S MASKING TAPE. Narrow and wide widths will help with this project.

4| PRIMER. An enamel undercoat primer is important if you're painting on bare wood.

5| PAINT. Use satin or semi-gloss enamel in the bathroom because it's easier to clean than flat paint.

6| GLAZE. All three of the decorative treatments we chose required latex glaze. You don't need a lot, so buy the quart size if available.

7| NEW HARDWARE. You may want new hinges, knobs, or pulls. Be aware that if the new hardware's screw holes don't match those of your existing hardware, you will need to drill new holes. Hinges can be difficult to set, so try to buy ones that match your old hinges.

8| DISPOSABLE GLOVES. Buy a box of 100. They're cheap and save lots of hand-scrubbing time.

9| VARNISH. An acrylic varnish is the best way to protect painted finishes.

10| PATCHING COMPOUND. Also called spackling compound. Buy a small container of the quick-drying lightweight indoor variety to fill old screw holes as well as dents and gashes.

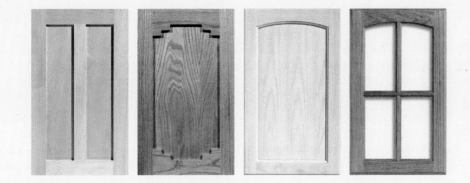

UPGRADE

If simply changing the finish of your cabinet isn't dramatic enough, order new doors and drawer fronts in the desired style. Get them unfinished and paint them when you do the cabinets.

▶ **DO IT RIGHT**

Use liquid sandpaper (also known as chemical deglosser) to ensure a good bond over varnished surfaces. It's especially effective on hard-to-sand fluted or carved surfaces.

+ WHAT CAN GO WRONG

If you're painting an unfinished cabinet, knots can bleed through the final finish over time. To prevent this, brush a shellac-based sealer over the knots before priming the cabinet.

Prepare for Paint

1 **EMPTY THE CABINET AND REMOVE THE DOORS AND DRAWERS.** Remove all hardware, including hinges, and keep them safe in a bucket if you plan to reuse them later. (If reusing the old hardware, as we did with two of our treatments, you may need to use steel wool to remove rust. Then use a rust-inhibiting primer before painting the pieces.) Protect the floor by spreading a canvas drop cloth over a layer of paper or plastic sheeting.

2 **SAND LIGHTLY.** You only need to degloss the finish, not remove it, so sand lightly. A random-orbit or palm sander speeds the work, and sponge sanders get into detailed areas, such as on raised-panel doors.

3 **MASK AND PRIME.** Mask off the walls around the cabinet and the cabinet rails and drawer front edges, too. Then apply a quality enamel undercoat primer with a brush to ensure compatibility between the existing finish and the top coat.

4 **FILL HOLES YOU'LL NO LONGER NEED.** If your new hardware won't fit into the existing holes on the cabinet base, doors, and drawers, press patching compound into unused holes with a putty knife. A second coat is often required; in that case, allow the first coat to dry, then sand it lightly with a fine-grit sandpaper before you apply an additional coat.

Combing & Antiquing

There are many ways to decoratively paint your cabinet, two of which are suggested here: combing (steps 5 and 6) and antiquing (steps 7 and 8). The final results are shown on pp. 25 and 34 (right).

5 **APPLY TOP COAT COLOR.** Brush on the top coat, then use accent colors to add some pop. (We used a gloss white enamel top coat and bright green on the door panels.) Painter's tape ensures a neat job. Get a tight tape seal by running a plastic credit card over the tape's edge.

6 **COMB THE RAISED PANEL.** Start by mixing the color (1 part paint to 3 parts glaze) and applying it with a brush to the surface you want to comb. Then drag a rubber painter's comb over the surface in either straight lines or in wavy patterns as on the door panel shown here.

7 **START ANTIQUING.** Begin with single coats of varying colors. We used a deep red followed by blue-grey and overcoated with a deep cream color. Varnish between coats and allow each coat of paint or varnish to dry before proceeding to the next.

8 **SAND LAYERS TO COMPLETE THE ANTIQUE EFFECT.** Use 100-grit and then 150-grit sandpaper to remove paint and to reveal the hidden paint layers. Concentrate on areas that would normally receive wear, such as around hardware and at the cabinet base. When you're done sanding, brush on a solution of 1 part burnt umber (available in acrylic artist's tubes) to 4 parts glaze. Allow the umber glaze to collect in areas that would normally become soiled, such as in grooves, at door edges, and around knobs.

5 6
7 8

If you don't like what you've done when sponging, combing, or creating other techniques with glaze, simply wipe off the glaze with a damp rag before it dries.

✳ DO IT FAST

Painting small objects, such as knobs, is quicker and easier if you screw them onto a sheet of scrap cardboard before brushing or spraying them. Leave enough space between the knob and cardboard so you can reach the undersides.

Sponging & Spattering

Sponging (steps 9 and 10) and spattering (step 11) are two more decorative paint techniques that can transform your vanity cabinet.

9 **PREPARE TO SPONGE.** Choose two or three colors that go well together. We chose a muted green as the base color and sand as the sponge-on color. Use a brush to apply the base color to the surface you want to sponge. Halve the sponge with a utility knife, then cut one of the halves in two so that you end up with one large piece and two smaller pieces. Cut the sponge so that one side of each piece is flat.

10 **MIX PAINT AND APPLY SPONGE.** Mix 1 part sponge-on color and 4 parts glaze in a bucket and pour it into a paint tray. Lightly load the flat side of the sponge. Tap off excess paint and blot the sponge on a paper towel, then lightly press it to the surface receiving the decorative treatment. Avoid excessive overlapping and rotate the sponge to avoid repetitive patterns. Use the larger piece of sponge for broad flat areas and the smaller pieces for tight corners. Reload the sponge as soon as the imprints become hard to see; continue until the surface is covered.

11 **DECORATE KNOBS.** Enhance wooden knobs with spattering. Prime the knobs and then apply the base coat color used for your cabinet. Cover the area so you don't spatter everything. Then cut an inexpensive China bristle brush so that ½ in. of bristle remains. Load the brush lightly with an accent color. Spatter the knob by drawing back the bristles and releasing.

12 **INSTALL NEW HARDWARE (OPTIONAL).** If you decide to replace knobs and pulls, use a combination square to measure and mark for the new holes. Be sure to use the same measures for each door and drawer! Drill the new holes, using a drill bit slightly larger than the screws you'll be using. Then screw on your knobs and pulls. Buy replacement hinges and install them in the original hinge holes.

9 **10**

11 **12**

Styles come and go—and come back again! Using a decorative paint treatment is a quick and easy way to change the look of your bathroom. Switching out hardware completes the style transformation. On these pages we illustrate two alternate decorative paint treatments in very different styles on the same vanity.

Antiquing makes new furniture look even better than old. The trick is to be sure the base coat colors complement the top coat. The inexpensive looks-like-glass hardware completes the transformation. Save money and have some fun by mixing reproduction knobs with the original wood knobs (detail, left), distressed to match the cabinet.

Tired of the traditional vanity? Convert a piece of furniture to serve the purpose. Here, an old dresser does the job nicely. The drawers were dismantled but the fronts were left in place. The top drawer front pivots forward for storage of small items, and the bottom two drawer fronts are joined to form a door. The finish is crackled.

Sponging, done with restraint, can look elegant. Choose the right hardware and the effect can be stunning. Other knob and pull options include the spattered approach (top right) and a more contemporary look (bottom right).

Helpful Hang-Ups

Put bathroom walls to work by installing **BARS, HOOKS & PEGS**

THE SELECTION AND PLACEMENT of relatively small fittings, such as soap dishes, robe hooks, and towel bars, can have a big impact on how well your bathroom functions. There's nothing worse than spending thousands of dollars remodeling your bathroom only to end up with an awkwardly placed toilet paper holder or a towel hook that's just out of reach of the shower. These little items can affect the design personality of your bath as well. Whether you choose a suite of similarly styled hang-ups or prefer to mix and match, you'll find an enormous selection at your local home center. Installation is a snap thanks to tools like the cordless drill and new stronger, easier-to-install wall anchors.

MEASURE & LEVEL   **MARK & DRILL**   **INSTALL THE ANCHORS**   **SECURE THE FIXTURE**

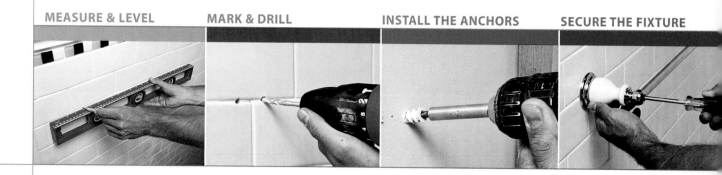

⊘ UPGRADE

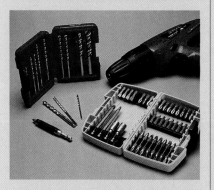

If you don't already own them, add a masonry drill bit set and a driver bit set with a magnetic bit holder to your collection. They allow you to deal with almost any installation more quickly than trying to get by with only a few bits.

✚ WHAT CAN GO WRONG

It doesn't take much torque, or power, to drive anchors or screws. Overdriving can break the drywall, making the anchor useless. Use a screwdriver if you're just installing a few anchors. For jobs with lots of anchors, you may want to use a drill/driver. Set the clutch to the lowest setting and drive slowly.

Tools & Gear

Just the basics for this project!

DRILL/DRIVER (PREFERABLY CORDLESS). Nothing beats the convenience of a cordless drill/driver. It's a worthwhile addition to any tool collection.

DRILL BITS OF VARIOUS SIZES. Pick up a drill accessory kit that includes quick-change bits and a magnetic bit holder.

RETRACTABLE TAPE MEASURE. A 16-ft. or 20-ft. tape with a 1-in.-wide blade is the most versatile and suffices for most do-it-yourselfers. The extra-wide blade is stiff when extended, allowing you to take longer unsupported measures.

SPIRIT LEVEL. Also known as a carpenter's or bubble level, this tool is available in several lengths. A 2-ft. level will do in most cases.

COOL TOOL

Hammer drills (also known as impact drills) are available corded or cordless. They add a fast hammering action to bit rotation. This feature speeds drilling in masonry and tile, as well as in wood. As a bonus, the bits stay cool so they last longer.

What to Buy

If you remove or relocate existing hardware, chances are you'll need to repair and paint a wall (see PREP PROJECTS on p. 20). Otherwise just pick up the following items:

1| BATHROOM ACCESSORIES. Design lines (suites) usually include a towel bar, towel ring, hooks, and toilet paper holders; some include cup holders and other accessories. When making your selection, keep function and safety in mind. Remember that bars allow towels to dry faster than hooks. And don't install anything where it could poke an eye in the event of a slip and fall.

2| WALL ANCHORS. Although hollow-wall anchors are typically included with accessories, they may not be right for your situation. Check the package contents before you leave the store so you save yourself a return trip!

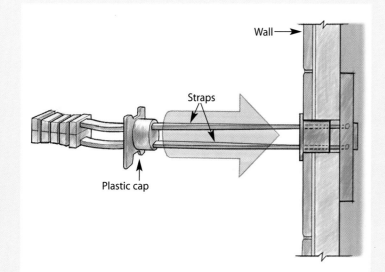

DO IT RIGHT

Wall anchors are needed when you want to attach an item to a surface that doesn't have solid wood behind it—such as in between studs on drywall or on a hollow-core door. For demanding accessories, such as grab bars, use anchors that provide a minimum of 250 lb. deadweight pullout. The Toggler® Snaptoggle® is one such anchor. To install it, simply drill the proper size hole in the drywall, plaster, or other hollow-wall material, using a masonry drill bit. Next, insert the anchor in the hole and pull it tight against the back of the wall. Then push the plastic cap against the wall and bend the straps to break off the excess. You're now ready to screw on your fixture.

To prevent a drill bit from wandering off mark when starting a hole in tile, nick the tile surface with a centering punch. Just a light tap, though, or you may crack the tile!

✛ WHAT CAN GO WRONG

Drilling into tile (or the grout joint between tiles) with a large-diameter bit may crack the tile. To lessen the chance of this happening, start with a 1/8-in.-diameter bit and increase the bit size one size at a time until you reach the proper size hole for the anchor.

Install a Towel Bar

1 **MARK THE LOCATION.** Using a tape measure and a level (or in this case a level that has a ruled edge and enables both tasks), mark the center points for the accessory's mounting plates. Hold a nail through the center of the plate to help position it on the marked center point. Then mark the mounting-hole locations, taking care to put the marks dead center.

2 **DRILL THE HOLES.** Drill holes as required for the type of wall anchor you are using. For drilling into tile, use a carbide-tipped masonry bit. Start with a pilot hole and work up to the the anchor hole diameter. For drywall, drill a test hole to find out if an anchor is required. If you're lucky and you hit a stud, you'll just need a screw to secure the mounting plate. If not, install a hollow-wall anchor.

3 **INSTALL THE ANCHOR.** In tile, press a heavy-duty expansion anchor, such as the Toggler® Alligator®, into the hole by tapping it with the heel of a screwdriver or a small hammer (inset photo). In drywall, press firmly on your drill/driver to slowly twist in a self-

tapping, coarse-threaded anchor. Set the drill/driver clutch at its lowest setting to avoid overdriving the anchor. Safer still, drive in the anchor with a screwdriver.

4 **SECURE THE ACCESSORY.** When all the anchors are installed, position the mounting plates and attach them with screws using a screwdriver or a drill/driver at the lowest clutch setting. Then attach your accessory. In this case, the towel bar attaches with screws. Other towel bars may be secured with small set screws using a hex key (also known as an Allen wrench).

1

2

3

4

There are a multitude of useful items that you can mount

to your bathroom walls, all of which can be installed using the skills shown in this book. When buying bathroom accessories, keep in mind that they are offered in suites (such as the one shown in our project), as well as in unusual one-of-a-kind designs. The former is easier to coordinate, but there are rewards for being daring.

Toothbrush and soap holders can be found in a style to match most bathroom fixtures. These models are fun to look at and functional, too.

A magnifying wall extension mirror is a good addition to any bathroom, but it is particularly useful if your vanity is installed without a large mirror over it.

Double towel bars (right) and triple versions (below) add space for hanging lots of towels—a good solution for small bathrooms that see a lot of use.

Accessories, such as these robe hooks, are available in more finishes than ever, from traditional chrome and brass to brushed nickel and antique bronze.

A one-armed toilet paper holder makes changing rolls easy.

Painted Wainscot Walls

Warm up your bathroom with easy-to-install **WAINSCOT PANELS**

WAINSCOT IS A POPULAR WALL TREATMENT in the bathroom because it is durable, holds up to abuse, and looks great. Panels are available in natural wood—like oak and birch that are ready to be stained, varnished, or painted—or primed MDF, a super-smooth manmade panel, which was used in this upgrade. The ¼-in.-thick, 7-in.-wide panels go up faster than individual boards and take paint beautifully. They are thin, so they fit behind toilets and vanities, and against door and window trim easily.

MEASURE & CUT   **INSTALL WAINSCOT**   **INSTALL TRIM**   **APPLY PAINT**

✦ DO IT NOW

Seal the back and edges of the panels with paint primer/sealer, and apply a first coat of paint on the face before installation. (Use varnish to seal and finish natural wood wainscot.)

▶ DO IT RIGHT

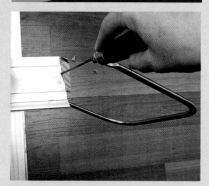

Use a coping saw to cut along the profile of a mitered piece of trim so it will fit over the piece you're joining it to. Test the fit, and use the coping saw or a round file to further adjust the cut until it fits against the installed trim perfectly.

Tools & Gear

You'll need most of the tools you keep in your all-purpose tool bucket, like a wrench, screwdrivers, drill, and putty knife. You'll also need these:

TAPE MEASURE. Buy a tape with a wide, stiff blade and big easy-to-read markings.

POWER MITER SAW OR MITER BOX AND FINE-TOOTH HANDSAW. The power saw may be worth renting for a half day when you are ready to install trim.

CIRCULAR SAW. Use it with a straightedge guide and clamps for cuts along a panel's length or with a quick square for crosscuts. Equip the saw with a trim blade.

JIGSAW. A tool that can make all types of cuts, it's the first saw to add to your toolbox. Or you can substitute an inexpensive keyhole saw.

SPIRIT LEVEL. Hold this tool against a surface to check for level or plumb—if the bubble is centered, you know it's straight.

COMPASS. This is the same tool you used to draw perfect circles when you were a child. In this project you'll be using it as a scribe.

SAWHORSES. For safe cutting, make a temporary work surface with a piece of plywood and a pair of these.

HAMMER. A 16-oz. straight- or curved-claw nail hammer is the most versatile.

BLOCK PLANE. Either a wood-and-metal or all-metal model is fine.

QUICK SQUARE. Sometimes called a Speed® Square, this tool is handy for marking 45- and 90-degree cuts and for use as a saw guide when making those cuts.

COPING SAW. Use this narrow-bladed saw for making fine cuts in molding, such as when coping a joint.

COOL TOOL

Sure you can use a hammer and nail set to drive and countersink hundreds of nails, but a battery-powered brad nailer gets the job done much faster without a single hammer ding or sore thumb. It also won't split the tongue on the wainscot or the ends of trim boards. This model nailer accepts $3/4$-in. to 2-in. 18-gauge brads. This tool is a worthwhile purchase if you plan on tackling several trim and woodworking projects around your home.

What to Buy

1| WAINSCOT. Primed white MDF (medium-density fiberboard) is best if it's going to be painted. For this bathroom, we chose precut, primed, 96-in. lengths (shorter lengths are also available). The tongue-in-groove joints on the panel edges (see inset below) align the panels automatically. Stack the panels with thin wood spacers between them (see below) for 72 hours so they can acclimate to your home's interior humidity.

2| TRIM KITS. A trim kit will include 8-ft. lengths of base and wainscot cap, but you can use stock moldings as we did for this installation. Buy lengths and quantities that, when cut to size, will eliminate mid-wall joints.

3| PANEL ADHESIVE. Used when wainscot panels are applied directly to the drywall. You'll need one tube for every 32 sq. ft. of wainscot.

4| FASTENERS. You'll need 1-lb. boxes of finish nails—4d for the wainscot and any shoe molding, and 6d for baseboard. If you are using a nailer, 2-in. brads will work for everything.

5| PUTTY. Buy lightweight spackling compound. It is less likely to shrink and easier to use than regular spackling compound.

6| PAINT. Use 100% acrylic-latex gloss or semi-gloss paint, preferably treated with mildewcide to prevent mold and mildew.

7| PAINTER'S TAPE. If the tape will be applied to wallpaper or freshly painted surfaces, be sure to use a low-tack painter's tape.

TRIM CUTS

Use a miter box and fine-tooth saw or power miter saw to cut trim. The three joints below are the most common.

Butt joint
Use the zero-degree setting on your miter box or miter saw for square cut pieces that butt against the door trim or a cabinet at 90 degrees.

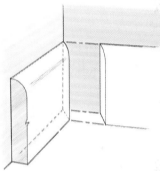

Miter joint
Cut 45-degree miters when two pieces will meet at an outside corner. Stand the board against the rear fence of the miter box or power saw, and use the 45-degree setting.

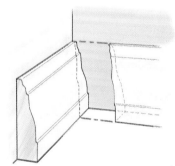

Coped joint
Cut a coped joint at inside corners (when using molding with contours). Square-cut and install the first piece. Then miter the second piece at a 45-degree angle. Cope as shown in DO IT RIGHT at left.

At all stud locations, nail through the face of the panels at the very top and near the bottom. (Apply putty to any nail holes that moldings won't cover later.) When there are no studs, nail at an angle through the tongue at four points (near the top, bottom, and at two points in between) to hold each panel tight against the wall while the adhesive cures.

After scribing a panel, use a jigsaw to make a cut close to the cut line and then finish it off to the line with a block plane. After a test fit, sand and touch up the paint on the exposed edge before installing the panel.

Install the Wainscot

1 **CLEAR THE ROOM.** Remove the toilet (see GET SET, p. 8). If the wainscot is taller than a vanity backsplash, remove the vanity, or loosen its screws, so you can slip the wainscot behind it. Shut off the water to the faucet and disconnect the water feeds, remove the screws that secure the vanity to the wall, and cut any caulk seal behind the backsplash. Remove any other interuptions in the wainscot area, as well.

2 **PREPARE THE WALL.** Pry off baseboard using a pry bar. Mark a level line on the walls at the desired wainscot height using a spirit level. Measure out from a known stud location (e.g. near an electrical outlet) to locate other studs. (See GET SET, p 11.)

3 **START AT THE DOOR.** Cut panels to the desired height (if necessary) and test-fit the first piece against the door casing. Then measure for penetrations, such as outlet boxes, applying measurements from the wall to the panel. Use a jigsaw to make the necessary cutouts. Apply panel adhesive on the wall, as shown. Hold the panel to your level line and nail it in place (see DO IT RIGHT at left). Do the same for additional panels, fitting groove to tongue as you go. When you near an inside corner, measure the gap, top and bottom, to find the width of the last piece. Transfer the measurements to a panel. Mark a cut line and cut along it with a circular saw and guide, as shown.

4 **SCRIBE AND TRACE.** When turning an inside corner, hold the top of a panel to your line, plumb and about ½ in. away from the corner. Open the compass at least as wide as the widest point of the gap between the boards to mark the cut as shown. This will allow you to fit the panel to an out-of-square corner. To mark the cut line at an outside corner, hold the panel in place, level to the layout line, and then trace a cut line onto the back side of the panel (inset photo).

1

2

3

4

Finish Up

5 **INSTALL CAP MOLDING.** Measure and cut the cap molding. We used a 1x3 to form a shelf and added a ¼-in. by ¾-in. piece of pine lattice to trim underneath (see TRIM CUTS, p. 47). Drill ¹⁄₁₆-in.-diameter pilot holes at 45-degree angles on the shelf at each stud location. Drive 6d nails into the holes and use a nail set to sink them slightly below the surface. Secure the lattice with 4d finishing nails. Be sure to drill ¹⁄₁₆-in.-diameter pilot holes when nailing near the ends to avoid splitting the thin wood.

6 **INSTALL THE VANITY AND BASEBOARD.** Reinstall the vanity before you measure for and cut the baseboard molding. Where possible, hold the trim in place to mark where it must be cut (inset photo). Use a miter saw and  miter box to cut baseboard joints. Fasten baseboard at every stud with two 6d finishing nails (or 2-in. brads if using a nailer). Work clockwise around the room. Some wainscot kits require baseboard to be installed before the paneling, so check your product's instructions.

7 **PUTTY, MASK & PAINT.** Fill any nail holes that will not be covered by moldings with fast-drying lightweight spackling compound and a putty knife. Use painter's tape to mask the trim, floor, and wall before you brush a final coat of paint on the wainscot and trim.

8 **PUT EVERYTHING BACK.** Reinstall towel bars (see HELPFUL HANG-UPS, starting on p. 36), switch and receptacle covers, and the toilet tank, reversing the procedure you used to remove them.

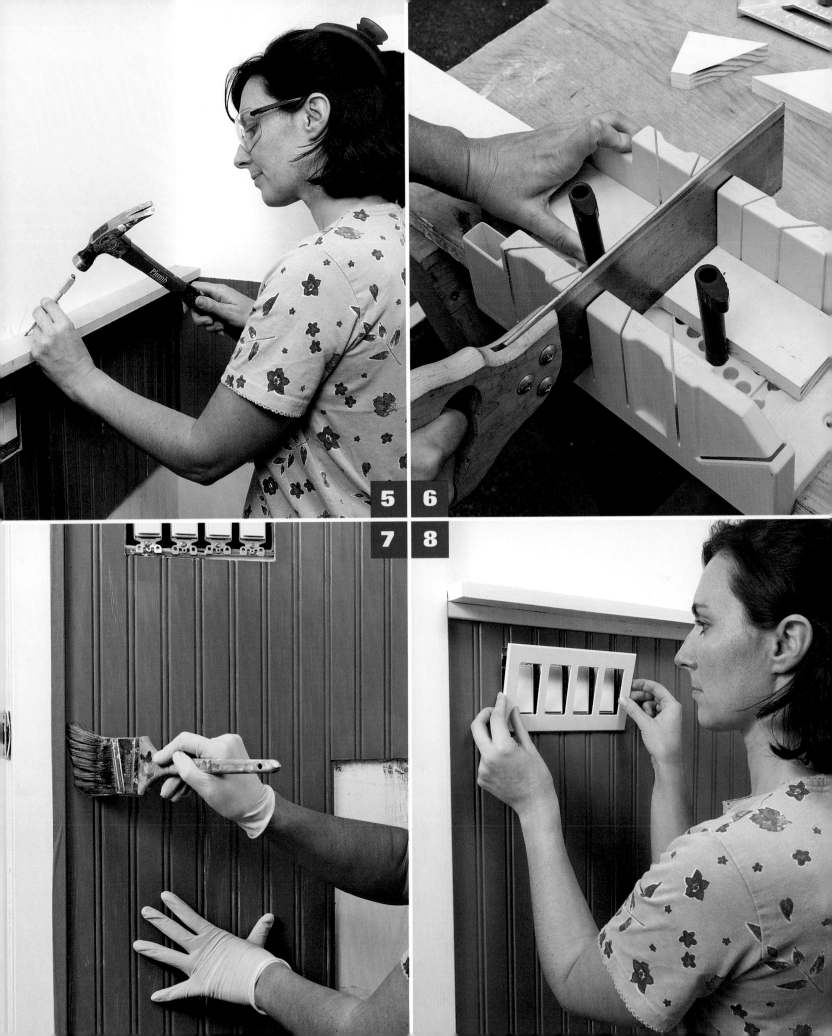

5 **6**

7 **8**

White trimwork pulls this spacious bathroom together. Beadboard paneling helps this bathroom to maintain a traditional feel, even with the large tub and glass-enclosed shower.

Use a shelf to cap your wainscot to create a handy place for small, decorative items.

Wainscot is a great way to unify a room visually, especially a room with lots of utilitarian fixtures, such as a bathroom. While beadboard panels are the most frequently used material, wainscot can be made from wider wood boards, ceramic or stone tile, and acrylic or other synthetic panels.

With so many styles and colors of border tiles available, combining them with wood creates a unique design statement.

For a cozy and traditional look, use bead-board wainscot on the walls and bead board on the ceiling.

Run bead board diagonally (top) for a more contemporary look, or choose tile board (above) for a low-cost alternative to ceramic tile.

Updated Vanity Lighting

Brighten up your bathroom with an easy-to-install **LIGHT FIXTURE**

HE RIGHT LIGHT FIXTURE can make or break a bathroom design, both from a visual and practical standpoint. Fortunately, replacing the light fixture is pretty straightforward and is something even a novice can do safely. With so many sizes and styles to choose from, the hardest part of this project is choosing a new fixture! So if you have a couple of hours on hand and want to add instant style to your bathroom, read on.

REMOVE THE OLD LIGHT   PREP THE SURFACE   CONNECT THE NEW FIXTURE   ATTACH THE TRIM

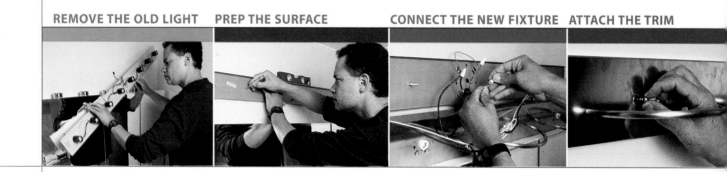

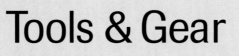
+ WHAT CAN GO WRONG

Be sure to choose a fixture that fits the space. Also make sure you use the right wattage bulb that's approved for the fixture.

+ SAFETY FIRST

Use a circuit tester to verify that the power is off before you begin wiring. To use it, touch one probe (lead) to any black or red "hot" wire. Touch the other lead to any white (neutral) or bare (ground) wire. If the juice is off, the tester light will not glow.

▶ DO IT RIGHT

Use a cable clamp to lock cables to junction boxes or fixtures and to prevent abrasion of the cable sheathing.

Tools & Gear

You may not need all these tools— it will depend on the existing fixture and wiring, and the replacement fixture you choose.

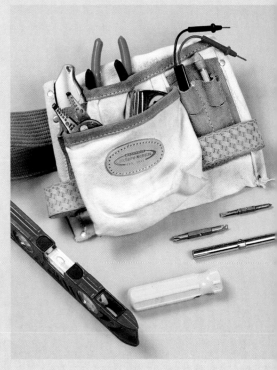

TORPEDO LEVEL. Select one that is magnetic to make leveling a fixture hands-free.

CIRCUIT TESTER. Never work on electrical wiring without this inexpensive tester.

6-IN-1 SCREWDRIVER. You'll be ready for any screw size—and even a couple nut sizes—with this handy tool.

LONG-NOSE PLIERS. Use to bend wire ends into hook shapes for fastening under screwheads.

LINEMAN'S PLIERS. Also known as electrician's pliers, this is the best tool for twisting solid wires together prior to installing a wire nut.

WIRE STRIPPER. Buy one with a wire gauge range from 10 (largest) to 18 (smallest). It will cover all your home wiring needs.

DROP CLOTH. Protect your sink and counter with a drop cloth, old towel, or blanket as you work. One slip, and a dropped tool could chip a sink or mar an expensive faucet.

STEP STOOL. Although your light fixture may not be very high, a step stool will allow you to reach it completely and safely.

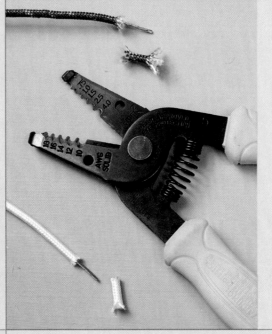

COOL TOOL

A **wire stripper** removes the insulating cover from the end of a wire so it can be twisted together with another wire or attached under a terminal screw as found on a light switch. It does this without nicking the wire, which is important because a nicked wire can weaken and break over time, causing a potentially dangerous short circuit. House wiring usually falls in the range between 18 gauge (such as lamp wire) and 10 gauge (large appliance wiring). To use the tool, place the wire in the appropriate cutter gauge, squeeze to cut the insulation and pull straight from the end of the wire.

What to Buy

Changing from side lighting to a single fixture over a mirror (or vice versa) often requires cutting open the wall, repairing drywall, and repainting. In addition to the extra work, it may require the services of an electrician. Keep this in mind when choosing your fixture.

1| LIGHT FIXTURE. Bar fixtures, such as the one we used, are often available in several lengths with various numbers of bulbs.

2| BULBS. Check the maximum wattage rating for the fixture. Most compact fluorescent bulbs typically will not last as long as claimed by the manufacturer.

3| TWINE. If you don't have a helper, use twine to temporarily hold a fixture while you wire it.

4| WIRE NUTS. These are usually supplied with the fixture, but you may need other sizes. It's wise to keep a few of each size in your tool kit.

INSTALLING AN OUTLET BOX

If you have a cable coming through the wall to your existing fixture and your new fixture must be mounted to an outlet box, don't worry. Cut a hole for a new "cut-in" oulet box (see photo) using a drywall saw, taking care not to cut into the cable. Strip the sheath off the cable to expose about 8 in. of wires, and insert the cable through the back of the box. (For more on this, see GET SET, p. 6.) Insert the box in the wall and tighten the three adjustment screws to lock it in place. Then attach a mounting bar to the box and screw in an appropriate length nipple. This assembly allows you to attach a fixture cover to the mounting plate. The nipple and mounting bar may be supplied with your fixture.

If you can't rest the fixture on the top of the medicine cabinet and you don't have a helper, temporarily hang the fixture from the fixture back plate with some twine.

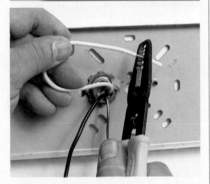

Always cut off the exposed end of an existing wire and strip off the insulation. The old wire end may be weak from wear so it's safer to get a fresh start.

Replace a standard switch with a dimmer. (See also GET SET, p 6.) Be sure to buy the right dimmer: There are models for low-voltage, fluorescent, and incandescent lights.

Replace the Fixture

1 **OUT WITH THE OLD.** Turn the power off to the lighting circuit. Protect your sink and counter with a drop cloth. Remove any globes and bulbs from the existing fixture, and unscrew any nuts that secure the fixture to the outlet box or back plate. Test for power with a circuit tester (see SAFETY FIRST, p. 56), then unscrew the fixture back plate from the wall, disconnect the wires, and remove the fixture. If the existing mounting bar and threaded nipple are the same as supplied with the fixture, keep them. Otherwise, swap them out for the new ones.

2 **PREP THE AREA.** Position the new fixture's back plate, level it, and mark mounting holes with a pencil. Drive a nail at these marks to see if any are over a stud. If not, drive hollow-wall anchors into the drywall and install the back plate. (See GET SET, p. 10.)

3 **CONNECT THE WIRES.** Cut off the exposed portion of the house circuit wires and strip off about ½ in. of insulation with wire strippers. Join the black and white circuit wires to their respective fixture wires by twisting them together and securing with a wire nut. Follow the manufacturer's instructions to properly ground the fixture. Typically you'll be instructed to connect a bare ground wire from the house wiring to the fixture's green ground wire. You may also be advised to loop the bare wire clockwise under a green grounding screw on the fixture's back plate.

4 **INSTALL THE COVER.** Gently fold and neatly tuck the wires between the back plate and cover (trim). Secure the cover with the decorative nuts provided. Install the proper wattage bulb(s) and any globe(s) or diffuser(s). NEVER touch halogen bulbs or any ceramic bases with bare hands—skin oil may cause them to explode only minutes after they are switched on. Restore the power and turn on the switch.

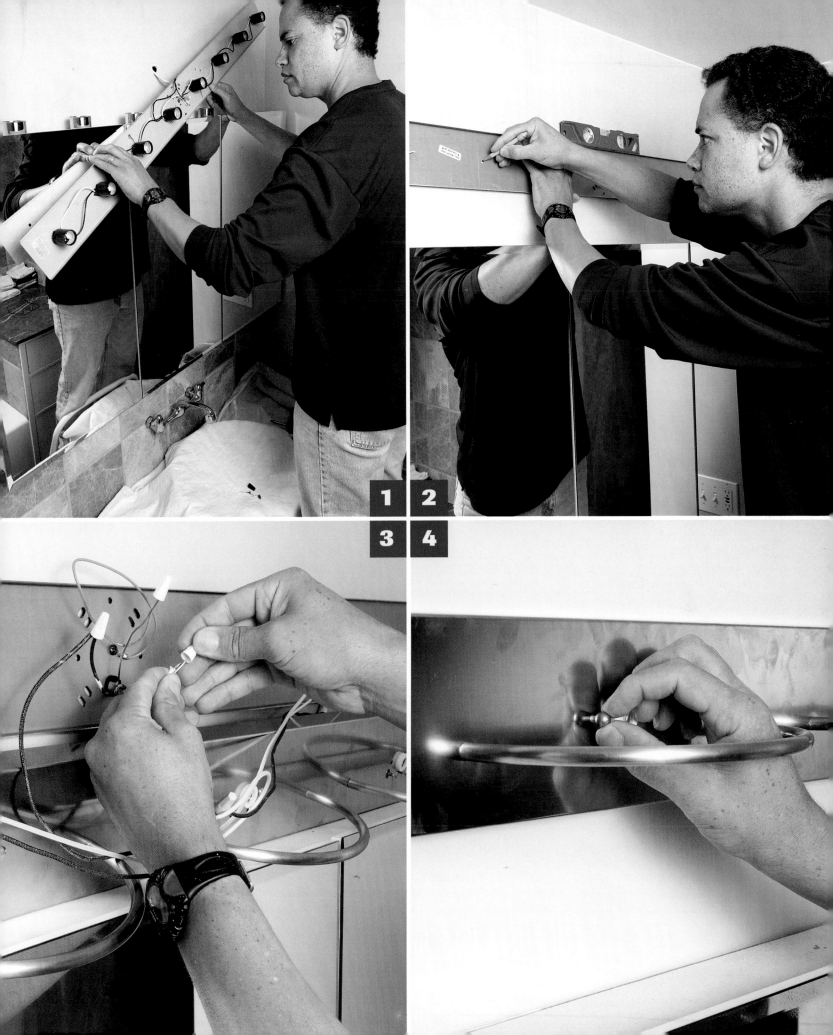

1

2

3

4

Choose fixture styles that enhance their settings. This rustic, wrought iron fixture is perfect for the Southwest flair of this bathroom.

A small bathrom is the perfect place to experiment with color and style. This retro bathroom features a whimsical accent sconce.

Lighting is both science and art, but most of us
buy a fixture based on its beauty. Fixture styles run the gamut from traditional to contemporary and can feature open or covered bulbs, multiple bulbs, colored shades, upward or downward facing bulbs.... You get the picture—there's a lot to choose from. Direction and intensity of the light is as important as how well the fixture fits with your decor though, so do your homework on the technical stuff, too.

The ideal way to light your face at a vanity mirror is with two eye-level lights with bulbs that are at least 60 watts each. An overhead fixture adds ambient light to the whole room, helping to light other spaces in a full bath.

Multiple light sources eliminate shadows when looking at yourself in the mirror. Here, the recessed overhead light combined with sconces on each side provide light just where it's needed.

Provide at least 75 watts overhead for each partitioned area of a bathroom, such as the tub area. The pair of fixtures flanking the window work well here, offering both a pleasing symmetry and an opportunity to halve the wattage in each fixture to create a restful space.

Flourescent lights are more energy-efficient than incandescent lights. They're not easily dimmed, though, so use them in a space where you want full voltage.

Glass Display Shelf

Add instant style and clutter control with a GLASS SHELF

WITH SPACE IN A BATHROOM AT A PREMIUM, shelves can do double-duty for both storage and display. Shelves come in all shapes and sizes—frameless, open, or closed, made from glass, wood, or one of a number of other materials. All you need to make a shelving unit work for you is the right space and the right shelf. So look around—you're sure to see a spot where you can install some instant organization and style.

MEASURE & LEVEL	INSTALL ANCHORS	SCREW IN THE BRACKET	ATTACH THE SHELF

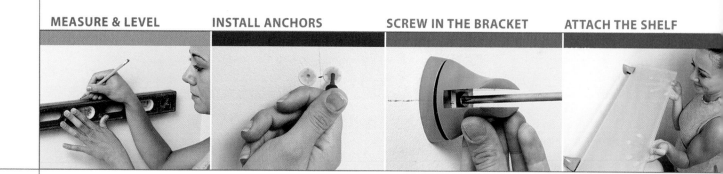

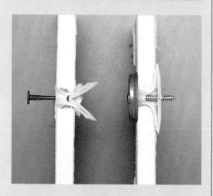

New types of hollow-wall anchors are easier to use and stronger than many older versions that are still sold today. Two noteworthy examples include the Toggler brand anchors (see GET SET, p. 10) and coarse-threaded screw anchors that don't require drilling a pilot hole.

✚ **WHAT CAN GO WRONG**

When is a level line not level? When your level is not accurate! To quickly verify a level's accuracy, place it on a surface you know to be reasonably level, such as a kitchen counter. Make a note of the exact position of the bubble in the center vial. Then flip the tool end-for-end. If the bubble is in the same position, the level is accurate. If not—and there are no adjustment screws— you're probably due for a new level.

Tools & Gear

Collect all the tools and supplies required for this project in a tool box or tote bucket to avoid unnecessary trips to the garage for tools.

SPIRIT LEVEL. This easy-to-use tool is a foolproof way to draw horizontal or vertical lines, or to check a fixture for level prior to installing it. A 2-ft.-long model suffices for most jobs.

DRILL/DRIVER. A drill that allows you to adjust the torque of rotating bits will give you better control when driving screws.

DRILL ACCESSORIES. At minimum you'll want to have the appropriate size drill bit for the anchors you choose to use. It's very helpful to have screw-driving bits and a magnetic bit holder, too.

STUD FINDER. Although there are other ways to find where the studs are buried in your walls, these electronic sensors will come in handy for this project and undoubtedly many others in the future.

RETRACTABLE TAPE MEASURE. A 16-ft. or 20-ft. tape with a 1-in.-wide blade is the most versatile and suffices for most do-it-yourselfers. The extra-wide blade is stiff when extended, allowing you to take longer unsupported measures.

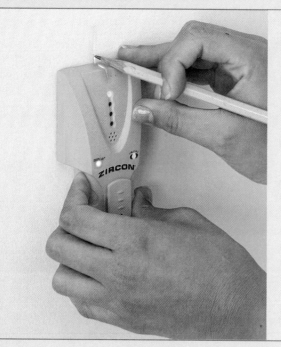

COOL TOOL

To locate studs in a wall or ceiling, you can look for slight depressions on the wall surface, measure from outlets, listen for a change in sound while tapping, drill trial holes—or you can invest in an electronic stud finder. Some models locate pipes and wiring, too. As you move the device slowly across the wall, a light goes on as it passes over the edge of a stud and off as it passes the other edge. Be aware that stud finders sometimes give false readings. They help but they're far from perfect.

What to Buy

These glass shelf systems are offered by several manufacturers and are available at most home centers. The shelves should be made of tempered glass for safety. Should they break, they will shatter into hundreds of pea-sized fragments that are relatively harmless compared to the falling shards of untempered glass.

1| SHELVING SYSTEM. Individual wall-mounted shelves are available in both traditional and contemporary styles and install in two basic ways: with wall clamps, such as the ones shown here, or shelf-length brackets (see DO IT FAST, p. 66). Finishes range from brushed chrome to brass to enamel colors.

2| ANCHORS AND SCREWS. When a system does not include these items, you'll have to buy them separately. Or you may prefer to use a type other than the one offered. Be sure it is equal to or superior in terms of how much weight it can hold.

INSTALLING OTHER SHELF SYSTEMS

Typically, the initial steps for installing most shelf systems suitable for a bathroom are the same as shown here. There may be differences, though, so be sure to read the manufacturer's instructions. Box shelves and cabinets that include open and closed storage may have a hanging rail—an integral horizontal board through which the cabinet is attached to the wall or wall framing. If so, you may need to drill clearance holes (holes through which the mounting screws will pass easily) with a countersink drill bit. Other types of shelves have hooks or similar hardware that simply hang on the heads of screws you drive into studs or wall anchors.

+ **WHAT CAN GO WRONG**

Erasing penciled layout lines and marks on a painted wall can leave smudges, especially on low-sheen and flat finishes. To avoid problems, make your marks only as dark as needed to see them and use only a clean, non-marring eraser. This artist's kneaded eraser works well.

✳ **DO IT FAST**

Installing shelves with wall clamps requires accurate measuring and clamp installation. For an easier, faster approach, use a straight bracket (above). Simply strike a level pencil line where you want the shelf, hold the bracket to it, and mark the holes for anchors or fasteners. With this bracket type, there's no chance of ending up with misaligned clamps that won't accept the shelf.

Install a Glass Shelf

1 **PLAN THE SHELF LOCATION.** Pencil a very light level line on the wall at the desired shelf location. Then locate the center point (we centered our shelf over the toilet). Now measure the shelf and halve the results. Use this dimension to measure from the center point and mark for the left and right ends of the shelf. Locate studs within these areas (see COOL TOOL, p. 64 and GET SET, p. 11).

2 **MARK THE MOUNTING HOLES.** The brackets should be installed equidistant from the ends of the shelf. About 3 in. to 4 in. for this 24-in. shelf looks good. Hold each bracket base in place to mark the mounting holes with an awl or nail. Be sure the center 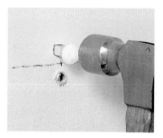 hole is precisely over the level line you drew on the wall. If there is no stud at a bracket location, install a suitable hollow-wall anchor for each screw (see DO IT RIGHT, p. 64). The Toggler brand plastic winged anchor we used is folded and tapped into a predrilled hole with a hammer. It supports 143 lb. when installed in ½-in. drywall.

3 **ATTACH THE TWO-PART BRACKET.** Attach the bracket base to the wall with the screws supplied with the hollow-wall anchor or, if there is a stud at the location, with coarse-thread drywall screws. Then secure the shelf clamp to the bracket base with the provided screw. Before going onto the next step, take a minute to erase any pencil marks on the wall (see WHAT CAN GO WRONG at left).

4 **INSTALL THE SHELF.** Insert the glass shelf first into one bracket, then the other. Some systems have rubber pads or tape that you place on the shelf or in the bracket before inserting the shelf. This one didn't. When the shelf is centered and fully seated, tighten the plastic setscrews (found under the brackets) to hold the glass in place.

1 2
3 4

Translucent glass is a pretty way to display objects or to hold the things you use every day, and its soft look complements most décor.

Mirrors in this bathroom reflect the natural light, making the room feel bigger and brighter. Shelves over the mirror add space for displaying collectibles, but they could hold more practical items.

Most bathrooms are small, so shelves can be a big help. Different types of shelves serve different functions. Closed shelves hide the necessities you don't want to look at, while open shelves can serve as both display space and holding spot for things you use every day. Look for shelves that do double-duty—some have a towel rack, some have cubbies, others have a mirror.

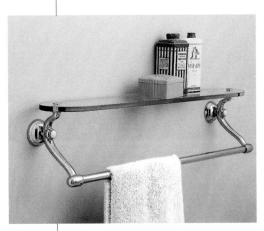

Look for shelves that have multiple uses, such as this shelf/towel bar.

If your bathtub doesn't have a shower component, use the extra space at one end to hang shelves for towels and other supplies.

Shelves offer a countertop area, which is especially important with pedestal sink designs that offer little counter space.

Installing a Tile Floor

If your bathroom needs a **NEW FLOOR,** tile tops the list for durability and creative possibilities

WITHOUT A DOUBT, TILE AND NATURAL STONE are the most beautiful and practical choices for bathroom floors. Large sizes and tight ⅛-in. spacing all but eliminate tile's biggest drawback: dirt-catching grout. Thanks to new tile backer boards and cool tools such as a tile wet saw, tiling a floor is doable for most homeowners. Floors with patterns take a bit more time due to extra planning and cutting. Your first step in this project is to take full advantage of a knowledgeable dealer for design, technical support, and materials. You can handle the rest!

| PREP THE FLOOR | LAY TILE | GROUT IT | APPLY SEALER |

Use only approved fasteners, typically either 1¼-in. roofing nails or 1¼-in. no. 8 by 0.375-in. HD self-drilling, corrosion-resistant, ribbed **waferhead** screws, and drive them flush with the surface.

When removing existing flooring, beware that pre-1980 sheet and resilient tile flooring and adhesive may contain asbestos. For testing and other information try your classified directory under laboratories or asbestos abatement contractors, your local or state department of health, or www.epa.gov/asbestos.

Tools & Gear

Common carpentry tools, such as a drill/driver, hammer, and prybar, may be required in addition to the following tiling tools.

SAFETY GEAR. You'll be on your knees a lot. Kneepads or a kneeling pad are a must! Wear eye protection when cutting, drilling, and hammering.

MARGIN TROWEL. For mixing small quantities of grout and adhesive.

SCORING TOOL. Sometimes called a carbide score and snap knife, this tool scores the surface of backer board.

CHALK LINE. Extend the chalk-covered string, hold the two ends against the floor, and then lift and release the line to snap a straight line between two points.

NOTCHED TROWEL. The notches ensure uniform adhesive thickness and distribution. The depth of the notch should be equal to about two-thirds of the thickness of your tile.

GROUT TROWEL. The firm sponge on this tool, which is also called a sponge float, works well to press grout into the joints and to wipe away the excess.

TILE NIPPERS. When curved cuts are needed, such as around a toilet flange or heating pipe, nibble away tile with this tool.

COOL TOOL

This **table-mounted tile saw** makes cutting tile easy. The tool consists of a motor-driven diamond-grit blade, a sliding table for the tile, and a 45-degree guide for diagonal cuts. A recirculating pump draws water from a pan and squirts it onto the spinning blade to keep it cool and to eliminate any dust while cutting. Have your rental tool dealer demonstrate how to use it safely. Some rental dealers may charge a "usage" fee for the blade but most do not. Avoid companies that ask you to buy the blade outright. Finally, be sure to bring the saw back clean to avoid unnecessary cleaning charges.

What to Buy

1| ADHESIVE. The one you use may vary with the type of tile you choose, so follow the tile manufacturer's and dealer's recommendation for type and quantity. Use this to adhere backer board to the subfloor and tile to the backer board.

2| BACKER BOARD. These panels are specifically designed for tile and are a must in wet locations. The Hardibacker® panel we chose has a grid that simplifies tile layout and is easier to cut and handle than cement backer board.

3| FASTENERS. Use 2-in. coarse-threaded drywall screws for reinforcing subfloors (1 pound will do it for the average 5-ft. by 8-ft. bathroom) and a 1-pound box of either $1\frac{1}{4}$-in. no. 8 ribbed waferhead screws or $1\frac{1}{4}$-in. roofing nails for securing the backer board.

4| TILE. Buy or order tile based on your drawing (see PLAN AHEAD, below). Purchase extras to cover mistakes and to have on hand for any future repairs. You may be required to buy full boxes.

5| TILE SPACERS. Pick up a bag unless your tiles have spacing lugs on their edges.

6| GROUT. Typically a "sanded" version is used for floors and "unsanded" for walls. Go over options with your dealer who can show you samples of dozens of colors and textures.

7| BUCKET & SPONGE. A large, firm synthetic sponge works best for cleaning tile surfaces after they are grouted.

8| SEALER. Grout, porous tiles, and natural stone flooring must be sealed for water and stain resistance.

9| SADDLE (OPTIONAL). Used for the transition between flooring materials at a threshold.

PLAN AHEAD

Finalize your tile layout and tile order on graph paper. Using a scale where $\frac{1}{4}$ in. equals 1 ft. works well. First, using the paper's gridlines as a guide, draw the tile pattern (here 12-in. by 12-in. tiles with four 4-in. by 4-in. accent tiles). Then draw two perpendicular layout lines across the paper (in red) that meet in the center of the paper (diagonally in this case for a diagonal tile layout). Now draw the room's perimeter, using the perpendicular lines as reference points. Draw in the position of the door threshold and vanity, too. (Typically both layout lines are centered in the room so that the cut tiles at the walls will be equal. In this project, however, the decorative pattern is centered on the threshold, so one layout line is centered on the doorway not the room.)

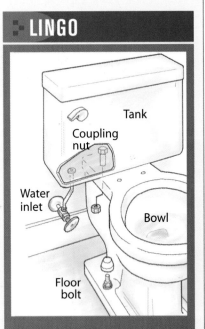

Prepare the Room

1 REMOVE THE TOILET TANK. Shut off the water below the tank, flush, and then sponge the remaining water out of the tank and bowl. Disconnect the water supply from the tank by unscrewing the coupling nut on the water inlet by hand or with groove-joint pliers. Using a large screwdriver, unscrew the tank from the bowl.

2 REMOVE THE TOILET BOWL. Pry off the floor-bolt caps with a flat-bladed screwdriver and remove the nuts that secure the bowl. If they are corroded, you may need to cut the bolts with a hacksaw (inset photo). Lift off the bowl and place it upside down on a padded floor. Put on rubber gloves to scrape the wax off the toilet and flange. Clean the toilet flange and the surrounding floor, and plug the hole with a rag.

3 REMOVE TRIM. If there is shoe molding along the baseboard, remove it using a trim pry bar. If there is no shoe molding, then remove the baseboard or plan to add shoe molding later. Use a piece of ¼-in. plywood or similar wood scrap to protect the wall from damage when you pry off the baseboard.

4 REMOVE THE EXISTING FLOORING. Remove the existing flooring using a floor scraper (unless it's well-adhered vinyl tile, which you can tile directly over). Apply heat with a heat gun to remove stubborn tiles. Then apply adhesive remover to soften the old adhesive so it can be scraped up. Follow the manufacturer's instructions for safety gear and ventilate the room well.

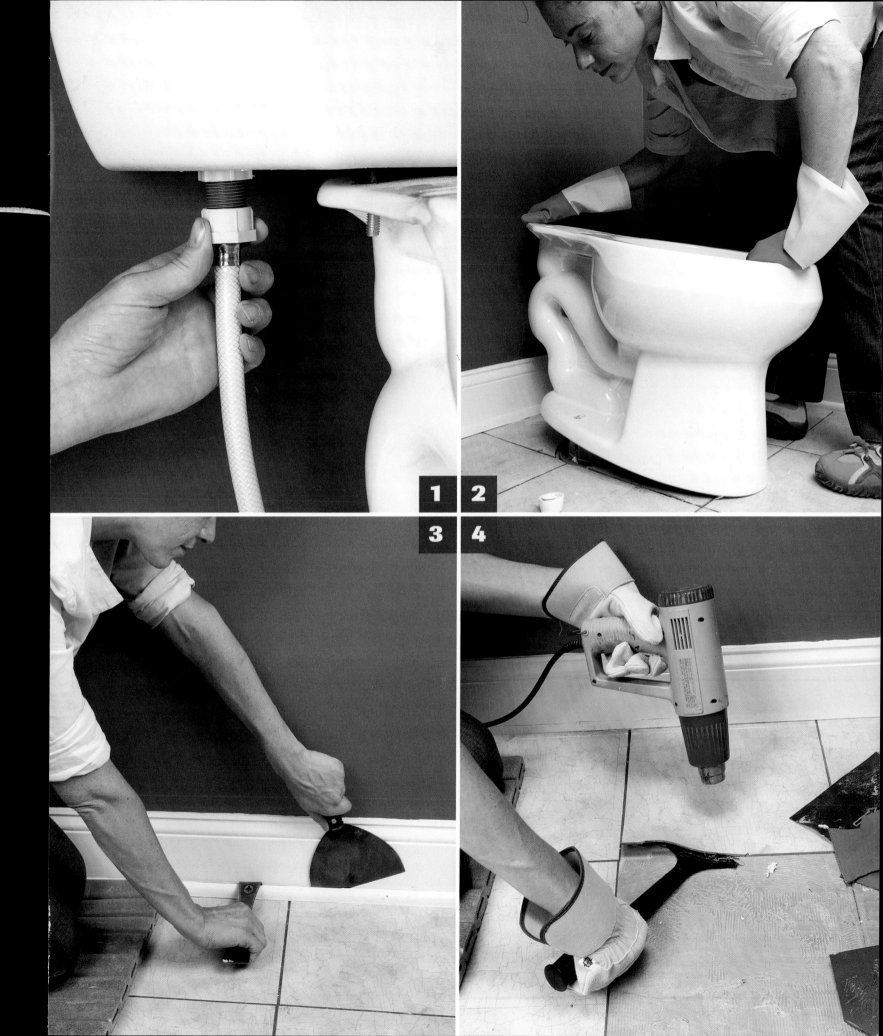

1

2

3

4

To cut the hole for a toilet flange score the necessary circle and score an "X" inside it. Place the panel on two boards positioned just outside the cutout area and break out the circle using a hammer.

To assure a good bond, vacuum and sponge-mop the surface of the backer board before applying the thinset setting bed.

Prepare a Proper Base

5 **ADD MORE FASTENERS.** To make sure the existing subfloor is as solid as it can be, drive 2-in. coarse-threaded drywall screws through it and into the joists below every 4 in. to 6 in. The existing nail pattern will clue you in to where the joists are. If you find rotted or uneven subflooring, it will need to be removed and replaced with plywood. Call a pro if you're not up to this task.

6 **CUT BACKER BOARD.** Plan your backer board layout, allowing for a ⅛-in. gap between panels and at cabinets and walls. Stagger joints so that four corners never meet, and don't align joints with joints in the subfloor. Score one side with a carbide score and snap knife, and snap the panel first away from and then toward the scored side. Test-fit all pieces. Mark panel edges on the floor as you remove them so you will know where to spread the adhesive.

7 **SPREAD ADHESIVE.** Mix adhesive according to the manufacturer's directions. Spread a thin (⅛-in.) layer of adhesive for one board at a time using the straight-edged side of a square-notched trowel. Hold the trowel at a 45-degree angle to create a uniform combed pattern in the final pass.

8 **INSTALL BACKER BOARD.** Fasten the panels, one at a time, every 8 in. in both directions. The grid on this panel makes spacing fasteners easy. Then, using the same adhesive, apply self-adhering fiberglass tape over the joints. First use a margin trowel to spread adhesive and fill the joints. Then embed the tape, remove the excess adhesive, and smooth the surface with the trowel. Allow the adhesive to dry overnight before installing the tile.

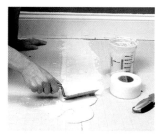

5

6

7

8

✦ DO IT NOW

There are two ways to begin laying tile. Either position tiles centered over each layout line or adjacent to each layout line. Use the starting point that yields tiles greater than a half-tile width at the opposing walls.

▶ DO IT RIGHT

Use tile nippers to cut curves, such as for a toilet flange. Measure from the last full installed tile to the center of the flange and transfer that measurement to the tile. Use a compass to mark a circle. Cut the tile into two pieces through the center of that circle and make closely spaced cuts with the tile saw in the section to be cut out. Then nibble away the waste.

❊ DO IT FAST

To fit a tile against a wall (or cabinet) place a tile directly over the last full installed tile and a second tile on top of it but against the cabinet. Then mark the cut on the first tile by tracing the edge where the second tile overlaps. If tiles are laid diagonally, use a combination square.

Plan & Cut

9 **SNAP LAYOUT LINES.** To create layout lines, measure the longest walls of the bathroom along the floor and mark the centers. Snap a chalk line through these marks. Mark the center of this line. Then position a carpenter's square at this point and snap a second, perpendicular layout line adjacent to the square. This divides the room into four quadrants (sections). Typically, both lines are centered, but you may decide to base your pattern on a fixture or cabinet. In our case, we centered the accent tiles on the door and between the vanity and toilet.

10 **INSTALL A SADDLE.** Set up a diamond blade tile saw, a rental item, and use it to cut a marble saddle to fit between the door jambs. The tile saw is messy, so use it outside or in a garage. Then use the saddle (upside-down) as a height guide when cutting off the stop molding on the door jamb with a handsaw. Spread a thin layer of construction adhesive on the floor and press the saddle into place, centered over the floor transition. Scrape off any excess and clean the saddle and adjacent floor with a damp cloth. Ask your tile dealer about other options for the transition between floors.

11 **LAY OUT TILES DRY.** Lay at least two perpendicular courses of tile that extend to the walls using tile spacers but no adhesive. Now you can determine how much will need to be cut from tiles at the perimeter—assuming your walls are square. (In this small powder

room using 12-in. tiles, we positioned all uncut tiles so we could do the cutting all at once.) Use a combination square and pencil to mark the cuts for the perimeter tiles (see also DO IT FAST at left).

12 **CUT TILE.** Cut the tiles for courses that abut walls or cabinets. Cut enough for one quadrant of floor at a time. Cut a curve to fit around the toilet flange (see DO IT RIGHT at left). Test-fit all tiles.

9

10

11

12

➕ **WHAT CAN GO WRONG**

Adhesive consistency is key to a successful job. Test by placing a tile in adhesive, pressing down, and sliding it about ½ in. to one side and back again. Use a trowel to pry it up and check for adhesive coverage. If there are voids, the adhesive is too dry. Add water and retest. Voids may also occur if the adhesive is not spread thick enough. You may need to adjust your technique or buy a trowel with a deeper notch.

▶ **DO IT RIGHT**

Place a straightedge on the surface of the tiles as you go to make sure tiles are even with each other. Make adjustments as needed until the tiles are perfectly straight and flat.

✦ **DO IT NOW**

Porous tiles, such as clay and some natural stone, can be stained by grout. Ask your dealer whether you should seal your tile before grouting in such cases.

Lay Tile!

13 **SPREAD ADHESIVE.** Mix the floor adhesive as you did in Step 6 and spread a liberal amount over a 10-sq.-ft. area in the quadrant farthest from the door. Use a notched trowel held at a 45-degree angle to comb out the adhesive in one direction.

14 **LAY TILE.** Starting at the intersection of the layout lines, carefully position the first course of tiles against the line, pressing firmly. Install tile spacers at the corners unless tiles have nubs for automatic spacing. Similarly install the remaining courses in the quadrant. You'll save time if you remove excess adhesive as you work. Keep a damp rag by your side for this purpose.

15 **LAY CUT TILES.** When all full tiles in the first quadrant are in place, install the cut tiles and mosaic insets. Then follow these instructions to install tiles in the remaining quadrants. Once all tiles are installed, let the adhesive dry overnight—and don't walk on the floor.

16 **REMOVE EXCESS ADHESIVE.** The next morning, remove the spacers (a screwdriver may help here) and wipe down the floor with a dampened piece of fine steel wool to remove any remaining adhesive on the tile surfaces. Use a utility knife to remove any excess adhesive from the joints. Finish preparing for grout by thoroughly vacuuming the floor.

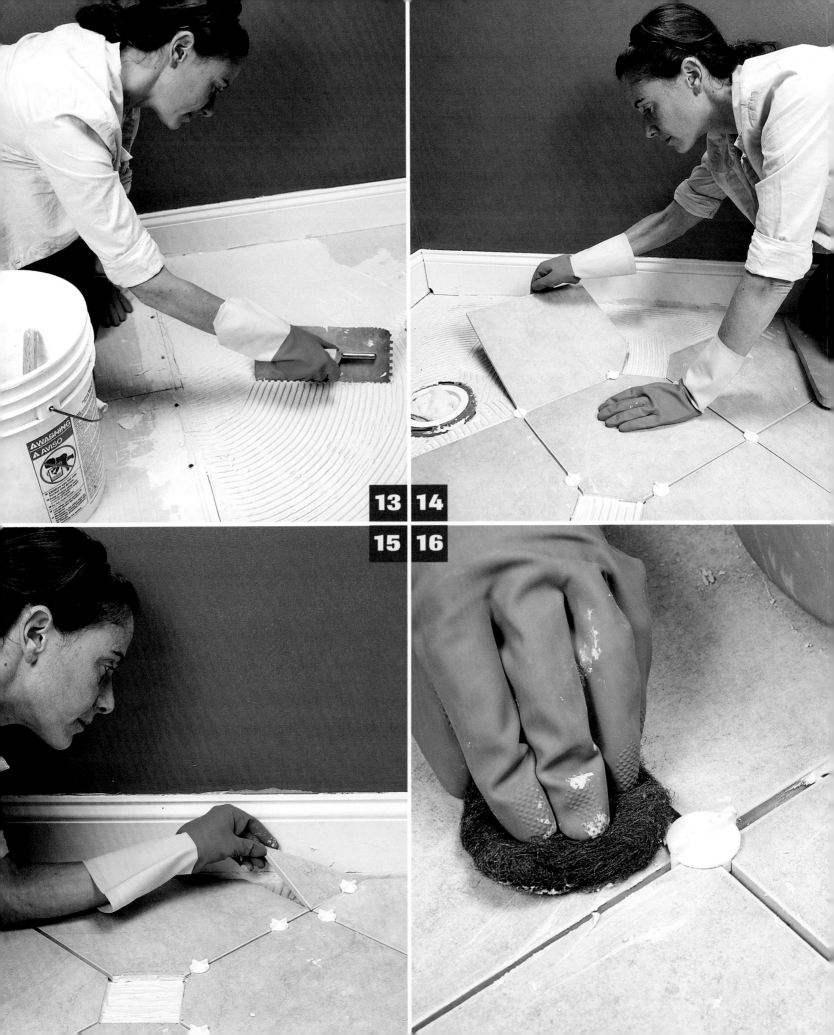

13 **14**

15 **16**

Grout & Finish

17 **MIX GROUT.** Mix enough grout to do the entire floor at the same time. Add the dry ingredients to the water according to the package directions and mix with a margin trowel. Allow it to rest undisturbed (called slake) for 10 minutes and remix, adding a little more liquid if needed. Allow to slake again. It should be just stiff enough that it won't pour out of the container.

18 **APPLY GROUT.** Start with the section farthest from the door. Press the grout into the joints with a rubber float held at about a 30-degree angle. Press firmly and spread until every nook and cranny is full. Then wipe off the excess grout, holding the trowel at nearly a 90-degree angle. In both cases, work diagonally to the joints so you don't rake grout out of them.

19 **CLEAN THE TILE SURFACES.** When the grout is stiff enough so it is not easily disturbed (about 15 minutes), remove any grout on the face of the tiles by wiping them lightly with a large, damp sponge. Rinse the sponge frequently and be sure to wring out all water  each time. Never allow grout to dry on the tile surface—it is nearly impossible to remove! After a couple hours, polish off the haze with a soft, dry cloth.

20 **APPLY SEALER.** Wait 72 hours, or for the time recommended by the manufacturer, and seal the grout joints (as well as natural stone or porous tile). It will make the floor more water resistant and less likely to stain. Don't skimp! Flood the floor with sealer, spreading it with a mop or sponge. Wait 10 minutes to wipe up excess sealer with a dry cloth. Reinstall baseboard or shoe molding to cover the cut tile edges.

17 **18**

19 **20**

Tile is timeless.

Its design versatility—and practicality—makes it the perfect choice for a bathroom. Tile can help unify a room or can be used in a way that makes it the focal point. Be sure to do your homework before choosing tile, though—there are literally hundreds of different sizes, types, styles, and colors to pick from. And don't forget about the grout; it can alter the look of a design based on its color and the width of the grout lines.

Mesh backings make installation of small tiles, decorative insets, and borders much easier than setting the tiles individually. Add these for a creative touch—and use them sparingly to keep costs in line with your budget.

This bath features tumbled marble tiles, where all the surfaces and edges have been abraded for a soft, matte finish. A gray grout was selected to match the gray tones in the marble. To make a real statement in your bathroom, apply tiles to the tub surround and walls, as was done here.

Large tiles, especially when set diagonally, can make a small bath seem bigger. Small tiles, as shown here, create a more cozy look. More grout lines, however, mean more maintenance.

Polished marble gives a formal look. It's beautiful but very slippery when wet. Mosaic insets (see detail photo), grouped in diamond shapes at every other corner, add interest.

Installing large areas of small tiles is a lot easier with pre-assembled sheets. The borders are preassembled, too.

New Cabinet Space

Install a new **MEDICINE CABINET** to give yourself lots more room for bathroom essentials

NEED A PLACE TO STORE all the gear you don't want to leave out in the bathroom? This surface-mounted cabinet can help! It has double the capacity of many recessed units and dramatically updates the look of your bathroom. If you have an existing recessed cabinet in an exterior wall, replacing it with a surface-mounted version will allow you to insulate behind it, tightening up a drafty spot. This is also a good project for practicing your drywall patching skills since the new cabinet covers the patch. To complete the transformation, consider adding a new light fixture.

MARK THE WALL   **INSTALL THE SCREWS**   **HANG THE CABINET**   **INSERT THE SHELVES**

NEED A HAND?

Get someone to help you temporarily position the cabinet to determine the optimum mounting height. For a family bathroom, that often means a compromise between what would be ideal for tall and short family members.

✓ UPGRADE

If you have a charger for an electric razor or toothbrush, keep it off your vanity and out of sight by installing a cord grommet in the side of the cabinet. A two-part cord grommet installs easily in a hole drilled with a hole saw (above). Clamp a backer board to the inside face of the cabinet to prevent splintering as you cut the hole in the cabinet (below).

Tools & Gear

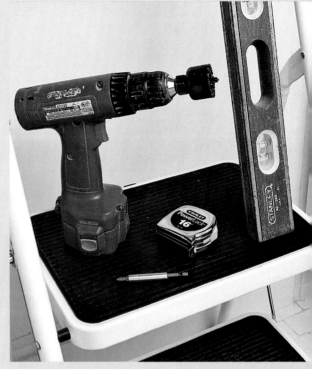

TAPE MEASURE. Buy one that's at least 16 ft. long with a ¾-in.- or 1-in.-wide blade that stays stiff when extended. Also, make sure that you can read the markings easily. Measuring mistakes can be costly!

2-FT. SPIRIT LEVEL. A spirit level typically has three vials: one in the center for checking level (true horizontal) and two for checking vertical. The 2-ft.-long model is probably the most versatile and is a good choice for your first level.

DRILL/DRIVER. You'll need to bore holes for wall anchors and to install screws, so make sure you have bits for both drilling and driving. A magnetic bit holder makes bit changes faster and easier. For plaster walls, you'll need carbide-tipped masonry bits for drilling.

STEP STOOL. Overreaching causes accidents and injuries. Use a step stool to stand on or to help you get up onto the counter when lifting the cabinet into place. Knee pads make kneeling on the vanity top much more comfortable!

HOLE SAW. This drill accessory will cut the large-diameter hole for the optional cord grommet (see UPGRADE at left).

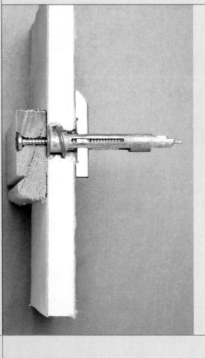

WHAT CAN GO WRONG

Although there are many types of hollow-wall anchors that will easily support the weight of a medicine cabinet and its contents, anchors that do not lock behind the drywall can work loose over time as the cabinet door is operated thousands of times. You also need to provide for the possibility that someone might foolishly pull on the cabinet when, for example, climbing onto the counter to change a light bulb. For these reasons use a self-drilling toggle, such as the one at left, that draws a substantial backing bar against the back of the drywall as it is tightened (see also GET SET, p. 10).

What to Buy

1| CABINET. Consider style, your storage space needs, and whether a surface-mounted cabinet will work in your existing space.

2| WALL ANCHORS. Anchoring cabinets and the like to studs is preferred but not necessary thanks to heavy-duty, easy-to-install hollow-wall anchors that lock behind the drywall. You'll need two to six, depending on the size of your cabinet.

3| FASTENERS. If you are fastening directly to a stud, you won't need a wall anchor. Instead use 2½-in. coarse-thread drywall screws. Wall anchors typically come with the appropriate screws.

4| CORD GROMMET. To install this optional accessory (see UPGRADE at left), you'll need to add a proper-size hole saw to your shopping list.

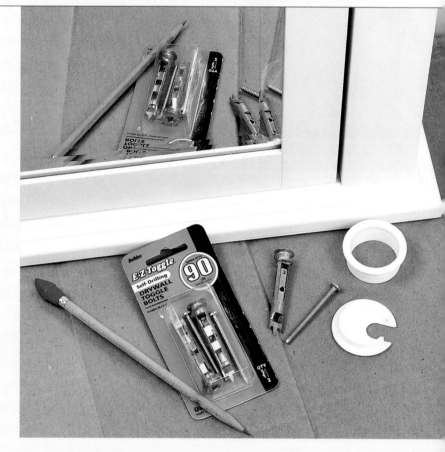

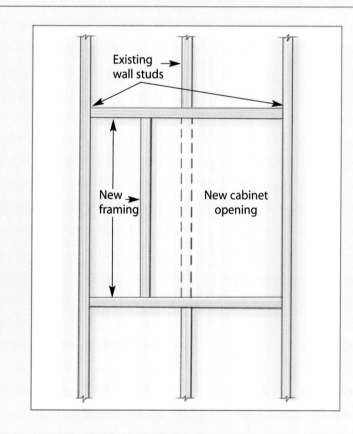

Existing wall studs

New framing

New cabinet opening

WHEN TO CALL A PRO

Reframing for a recessed medicine cabinet typically involves opening the wall, cutting away a section of one stud, and adding two new horizontal framing members and one new vertical member. It may also mean patching drywall and repainting. If you don't feel comfortable doing this kind of work, consider hiring a carpenter to prepare the opening. Then paint the wall and install the cabinet yourself.

Install the Cabinet

1 **MEASURE & MARK.** Mark the cabinet top's back edge at its center point; this will be the reference point when determinng the location of the mounting brackets. Then use a level and pencil to draw a vertical centerline on the wall. Draw it long enough so it will extend about 1 in. above the cabinet when it is installed. Choose where the top of the cabinet will be, then draw a level line on the wall where the top of the keyhole mounting hardware will need to be located. Mark the mounting-screw locations on the level line (inset photo).

2 **INSTALL THE MOUNTING SCREWS.** Shut off power to the room (see SAFETY FIRST at left). Drive a 2-in. mounting screw at each marked location. If you are lucky enough to hit a wall stud, just drive in the screw, leaving the screw head about ¼ in. above the surface.  If you don't hit a stud, install a hollow-wall anchor. Drive the anchor, such as an EZ Toggler®, into the wall. Then drive the supplied screw into the anchor to lock it against the drywall (see also WHAT CAN GO WRONG, p. 88). If you are going to install a cord grommet (see UPGRADE, p. 88), do it now before taking the next step.

3 **HANG THE CABINET.** Stand on a step stool so that you can see the top back edge of the cabinet as it is installed. Lift the cabinet up onto the wall, using the marked centerlines on the cabinet and wall to help you align the keyholes over the screws. Check the cabinet for level; if askew, reinstall all mounting screws at a slightly different height.

4 **INSTALL THE SHELVES.** Insert shelf supports at the desired heights into the predrilled holes inside the cabinet. Tilt the glass shelves as needed to place them on the supports. Erase penciled centerlines on the wall and cabinet and you're ready to load the cabinet. If you've installed a cord grommet, remove the slotted grommet cover to pass through the cord plugs, then reinsert it.

Medicine cabinets are the best place to store those small but critical items, such as thermometers, nail clippers, and aspirin. They keep everything at eye-level where you can spot what you're looking for quickly. Find one that suits your style—contemporary or traditional, surface-mounted or hidden to blend in with the walls. Take this opportunity to make a statement, whether your bathroom is small or large.

If the wall space above your sink is cramped, consider a recessed (shown) or surface-mounted cabinet placed over the toilet.

For a traditional look, wooden cabinets with framed doors are ideal. This unit, which can be surface-mounted or recessed, features a drop-down glass door in front of a display shelf.

Frameless mirrored medicine cabinets blend in with the wall and surroundings for a lighter, more contemporary look.

Hidden medicine cabinets are ideal when you want to minimize elements for a streamlined look. They can be painted or wallpapered to blend with any wall treatment. This unit has a steel door and can be ordered with a left- or right-hand door opening.

Surface-mounted cabinets are often designed to match surrounding cabinetry. Here each mirror panel opens for easy access to the contents. If you have small children in the house, it's wise to get a lockable cabinet.

Sink & Faucet Upgrade

For a makeover that's fun and fast, put in a **NEW FAUCET, SINK & COUNTERTOP** where the old ones used to be

OR MOST OF US, EVERY DAY BEGINS AT THE BATHROOM SINK. So why not freshen up what's already there? Changing a sink is pretty simple, especially if the replacement will fit the old opening or an enlarged one. And it makes sense to replace the faucet at the same time. This is easy to do if the faucet is mounted in the sink or if the countertop faucet holes match up with the new faucet. You may even want to replace the countertop. We will show you how to do all three.

REMOVE THE SINK   **CUT OUT THE OPENING**   **ATTACH THE FAUCETS**   **CONNECT THE PLUMBING**

A faucet must be well-secured to the sink or countertop or it will loosen up over time. For best results, use a spud wrench on the large-size nuts. It has wide adjustable jaws that lock in place when you tighten a thumbscrew. You could use groove-joint pliers (see GET SET, p. 9), but they can slip and so are not as safe to use as a spud wrench. A large adjustable wrench doesn't have the capacity for these large nuts. Due to the size of a spud wrench, it can only be used when the sink is removed from the countertop.

Tools & Gear

Actual tool requirements will depend on the extent of your project, from faucet-only to "the works."

TAPE MEASURE. Measure twice, cut (or drill) once.

CARPENTER'S SQUARE. Use this to mark perpendicular centerlines and to check inside wall corners for square.

PUTTY KNIFE. Buy one with a standard flexible blade to cut the caulk seal between a countertop and sink.

TRIM PRY BAR. This tool is stiffer than a putty knife and may be better for removing adhered backsplashes.

HAMMER. A 16-oz. nail hammer is the most versatile size to own.

JIGSAW. A scrolling model (one that allows you to turn the head instead of the whole tool as you cut) can sometimes get where standard jigsaws can't.

SCREWDRIVERS. Have an assortment of Phillips head and flat-blade screwdrivers on hand.

ADJUSTABLE WRENCH. This tool handles small nuts such as the one at the compression fitting of a shutoff valve.

GROOVE-JOINT PLIERS. With its small-to-wide capacity, you'll find it handy for many situations.

SPUD WRENCH. This tool, available in relatively inexpensive models, handles nuts larger than 1½ in. Groove-joint pliers may work, too.

CAULKING GUN. Sinks and backsplashes are adhered with caulk. The best guns have a quick-release trigger that stops the flow of caulk immediately upon release and a built-in tool for piercing the seal inside the caulk tube spout.

WHEN TO CALL A PRO

Solid-surface countertops and the undermount sinks that are often installed in them require professional installation. Although you can install a new faucet in this kind of countertop yourself, the connections may be difficult to access.

What to Buy

Check out the wide assortment of sinks and faucets online and download installation instructions, too. Then visit your local home center and/or plumbing supply outlet to make your sink and faucet choices. To familiarize yourself with proper installation (and verify there are no missing parts), follow the directions to pre-assemble the faucet without sealants.

1| SINK. If you are installing a new sink into an existing top, make sure the rough opening for the new sink is not smaller than the existing opening.

2| FAUCET. Choose from a convenient and relatively inexpensive one-piece single-lever model—or a two-handle model with either a 4-in. or 8-in. spread and a separate spout.

3| COUNTERTOP. Tops are available in a wide variety of materials, including resins and stone. Plastic laminate tops offer the most choices in colors and patterns.

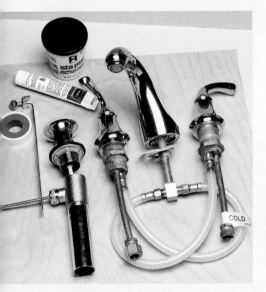

4| SUPPLY TUBES. Flexible reinforced tubes are the easiest to install when the feeds are not directly below the faucets.

5| SPRAY LUBRICANT. It makes corroded parts easier to remove.

6| PLUMBER'S PUTTY. This easy-to-work-with, non-messy sealant seals the joints between the sink drain and sink, and between the sink and countertop.

7| TEFLON® TAPE. This is one of two thread sealants you'll need. It wraps clockwise around male pipe threads.

8| PIPE-THREAD SEALANT. One small tube will do the trick.

9| ACRYLIC LATEX ADHESIVE CAULK. This type works for sealing the joints between the wall and the sink or sink counter, as well as to attach a one-piece sink/countertop to the vanity.

UPDATE YOUR COUNTERTOP, TOO

Measure the existing top and have a new one fabricated to the appropriate dimensions. If your vanity is to be installed in a corner or between two walls, order unattached backsplashes. Installed after the top, they cover any gaps at the walls should the room corners not be square.

Test-fit the top, then proceed with the installation. Put a bead of silicone caulk on the top edges of the vanity and position the top. You may also screw through the vanity corner braces into the underside of the top. Then squeeze a generous bead of silicone caulk on the back of any separate back or side splashes and press them firmly into place. Brace them overnight with precut boards against an opposite wall or a board clamped to the edge of the countertop (see photo).

DO IT NOW

If the sink to be removed has been set in caulk, break the adhesive seal with a putty knife. Tap the knife with a hammer to insert the blade between the sink and countertop. Then work your way around the perimeter until the sink is loosened.

DO IT RIGHT

Drill a hole then cut a hand hole in the center of a new countertop so you will be able to grip the cutout as you steer the saw over to cut the perimeter.

Out with the Old

1 **DISCONNECT THE EXISTING PLUMBING.** Place a plastic bucket under the drain to catch any water as you loosen the nut that secures the P-trap to the tailpiece (inset photo). Disconnect and clean the trap. Plug the drain hole in the wall with a rag. Then shut off the water supply valves under the sink and loosen the nuts that secure the supply tubes to the valves using an adjustable wrench.

2 **REPLACE THE EXISTING TOP (IF APPLICABLE).** If you are replacing your vanity top, break the adhesive-caulk seal between the backsplash and wall with a putty knife or trim pry bar and remove any screws that may secure the top to the cabinet. Remove the sink before lifting out the assembly (see DO IT NOW at left). If the faucets are mounted in the countertop, remove the nuts that secure them with a spud wrench or groove-joint pliers. Then install the new top by setting it in silicone caulk. Seal any joint between the wall and countertop with a bead of caulk. (See also UPDATE YOUR COUNTERTOP, TOO, p. 97.)

3 **MARK THE SINK OPENING.** With a carpenter's square, pencil perpendicular reference lines on the countertop that indicate the sink's left-to-right and front-to-back centers. Cut out the template provided with the sink and tape it in place so its reference lines align with  yours. Trace the opening onto the countertop. Alternatively, place the sink upside down on the counter. Trace it onto the top, remove the sink, and pencil in another line for cutting about ½ in. inside the sink outline.

4 **CUT THE OPENING.** Drill a ½-in.-diameter hole to provide entry for a fine-toothed jigsaw blade, then cut the sink hole with a jigsaw. Hold the waste piece as you cut around the perimeter to prevent it from breaking off as you near the end of your cut (see DO IT RIGHT at left). Test-fit the sink. Make a couple of pencil marks around the sink edge on the counter to help you correctly position it later.

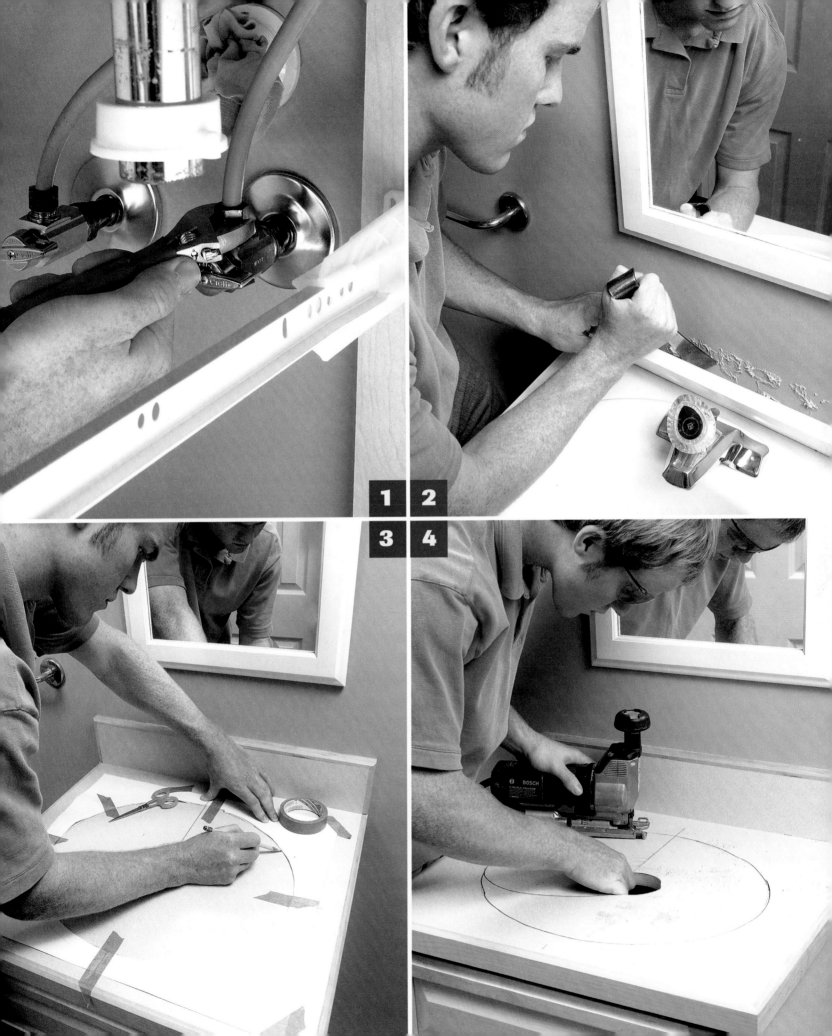

1

2

3

4

+ WHAT CAN GO WRONG

Don't over-tighten connections.
Contrary to what you'd think, doing so can actually cause leaks. Turn on the water and fill the sink to check drain lines, tightening them only as needed to stop any leaks.

✳ DO IT FAST

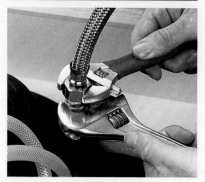

Flexible supply tubes, available in reinforced plastic or braided stainless steel, cost a bit more than the old metal or plastic ones but are easier to bend into position. Install them on the faucets before you install the sink to make connections to the house plumbing easier and faster.

In with the New

5 **PREP THE SINK.** With the sink upside down, install the faucet and drain assemblies using plumber's putty, Teflon tape, and pipe thread sealant as directed by the manufacturer. Plumber's putty is used for sealing the drain flange to the sink. When using it, roll it into a rope first to make the job go more smoothly. The former two sealants are used on water supply-line connections to prevent the tiny leaks that would otherwise develop.

6 **CONNECT THE STOPPER.** Insert the lift rod through the spout and, while holding the lift rod all the way in and the drain stopper pivot rod in the up (open) position, connect the rod to the stopper assembly with a thumb screw. Later, after the sink is installed, insert the stopper and adjust it as needed for the stopper to open and close properly.

7 **SET THE SINK.** While the sink is still upside down, make a large rope of plumber's putty and press it onto the underside of the sink rim. Then carefully lower the sink into the opening, setting the front edge first. Adjust its position per the reference lines you  made earlier. With a clean rag, remove excess putty from around the sink, the faucet, and the drain assembly and wipe these areas clean.

8 **MAKE PLUMBING CONNECTIONS.** Connect the plumbing by following the manufacturer's instructions and reversing the steps taken when you disconnected the faucet and sink. Attach flexible supply tubes to the shut-off valves and attach the P-trap to the drain stub-out (the fitting at the wall) and to the sink drain tailpiece (see photo). Hand-tighten and then tighten to snugness using an adjustable wrench for the supply-line connections and groove-joint pliers for the drain fittings. Turn on the water and inspect for leaks. If there are any, tighten connections one-quarter turn.

5

6

7

8

Vessel-style or top-mounted sinks can be mounted on everything from contemporary tables (right) to antique dressers.

Today's sinks are dropped into laminates and under-mounted in natural and synthetic stone countertops. Synthetic stone, also called solid surface, is available for single or double vanities and allows for edge treatments to complement your cabinetry.

Sinks and faucets go hand in hand.

Together they are a focal point of the bathroom. And the latest styles and materials mean that these very practical fixtures can look great, too. Check out the range of options: You're sure to find something in your budget and taste to upgrade your bathroom in a snap.

Seamless, one-piece sink/vanity tops leave no place for dirt and mold to collect. You can select from several edge treatments.

Faucet styles run the gamut from antique reproductions to the whimsical, such as this model that's reminiscent of old-fashioned water pumps.

Under-mounted sinks offer the opportunity to contrast materials and colors—and are also relatively easy to clean.

Acrylic Tub Surround

Replace tired tile walls with an **ACRYLIC TUB SURROUND** with built-in shelves

I F YOU'RE LOSING THE BATTLE to maintain an old tiled tub or shower wall, or just want to give an old bathroom a new look, an acrylic tub surround is just what you need. A tub surround kit is pretty inexpensive, and two people can complete the installation in a weekend. An added bonus—acrylic surrounds have few or no joints, so you'll no longer have to keep caulking the spots that have worn away or become discolored by mildew.

TEST-FIT   CUT PLUMBING HOLES   INSTALL THE WALLS   BRACE OVERNIGHT

Some people prefer the clean look of a three-piece unit over a five-piece unit, but your walls must be straight, square to each other, and plumb. Check them with a 4-ft. level and a carpenter's square before buying this type of unit.

A hole saw cuts clean, relatively large-diameter holes in wood, plastic, and other materials. It's the perfect tool for cutting holes for plumbing pipes in your surround. A hole saw consists of three parts: a cup-shaped bi-metal saw with a toothed or abrasive-grit cutting edge, a mandrel (with a $\frac{1}{4}$-in. or $\frac{1}{2}$-in. shank), and a pilot bit that guides the cut. The size(s) you need depends on your pipe and valve diameters.

Tools & Gear

Evaluate your existing tub or shower carefully to determine if you need additional tools to prep the surface before starting this project. This installation over tile, for example, required tools to remove the soap dish and some of the tile, and a sander to roughen the surface for the adhesive.

LEVEL AND SQUARE. A 4-ft. spirit level and a carpenter's square help you check whether your walls are plumb and square so you can plan adjustments to ensure the top of the surround is level.

SCREWDRIVERS. To remove faucet handles you'll typically need a Philips head screwdriver. Select the correct size to avoid slippage and damage to the screw head.

JIGSAW. Equipped with a fine woodcutting blade, this saw handles most of the cutting assignments for this project.

DRILL. Corded or not, almost any drill that accepts the $\frac{1}{4}$-in. shank of the hole saw will do the trick.

HOLE SAW. This drill accessory, a cross between a drill bit and a saw, simplifies cutting large-diameter holes for plumbing valves and pipes.

CAULKING GUN. Tub surround kits include 10.5-oz. tubes of adhesive so you'll need a caulking gun to use them. Make sure the gun has a quick release so you can relieve pressure and stop the flow of adhesive.

SAFETY GEAR. A dust mask and goggles are required when drilling and cutting. Also wear goggles when prepping the existing surface.

HAND SAW OR CIRCULAR SAW. You can use a handsaw to cut the wood braces, but a portable circular saw is best to cut plywood, if needed.

BAR CLAMPS. Fast-action, single-handed clamps with padded jaws are ideal for clamping the surround pieces while performing cutting, drilling, and shaping tasks.

HALF ROUND FILE. A double-cut model, which has two sets of parallel teeth in a criss-cross pattern, removes the materials quickly and smoothly.

SAWHORSES. Sawhorses assembled with brackets and 2x4s, such as the ones shown, break down for easy storage. They are a must for a project like this.

What to Buy

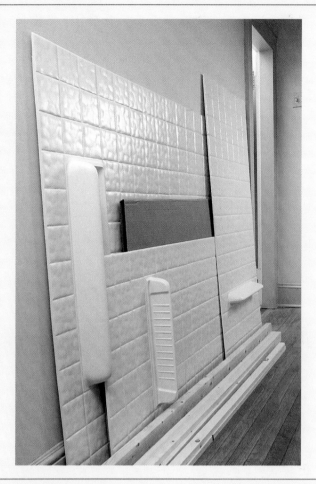

1| SURROUND KIT. Check the company's literature and your tub wall measurements to choose a model that will fit and that offers the features you want. This five-piece model fits tubs with end walls between 29 in. and 32 in. wide and with back walls between 57 in. and 62 in. wide.

2| MASKING TAPE. Use it when caulking and you'll never have a messy caulk joint again!

3| LUMBER. Lumber does double-duty. It's used to support the wall panels as they are cut, drilled, and shaped. Later on, with the panels in place, it's used to brace the surround while the adhesive dries. This installation required two 6-ft. pine 1x2s, six 6-ft. pine 1x3s, three 8-ft. 2x4s, a 4x8 sheet of 3/8-in. plywood, and two 8-ft. lengths of stop molding.

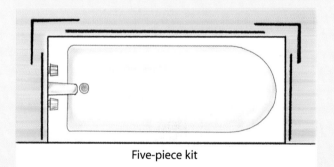
Five-piece kit

Three-piece kit

YOU GET WHAT YOU PAY FOR

Quality generally follows price when it comes to acrylic tub/shower surrounds. Better grade units will be thicker, easier to install, and generally have a nicer appearance. With thicker panels, manufacturers can offer surfaces with a more realistic tile appearance. You'll also have fewer problems with scratches and fading with a quality unit. The best units are made with solid surface (modified acrylic) panels or with molded acrylic linings reinforced with fiberglass. Lower end—and less durable—units are also fiberglass reinforced but have a baked-on gel coat. Pay close attention to the number, location, and design of the unit's shelves for soap, shampoo, and other shower items. In addition, some surrounds offer an extension kit that provides coverage to the ceiling. A five-piece kit will be easier to install than a three-piece one if your walls are not plumb or square, or if your tub is not level.

Prep the Surface

▶ DO IT RIGHT

Most tub spouts are threaded. If you can't twist one off by hand, insert the handle of a pair of pliers into the spout for added leverage, and turn counterclockwise.

◆ DO IT NOW

Although the new surround will be sealed at the tub, clean out old caulk with a screwdriver and re-caulk the tub/tile joint. The minor expense and time to have this leak-preventing backup is worthwhile.

✚ WHAT CAN GO WRONG

Acclimate the panels to room temperature for at least six hours before installation to minimize expansion or contraction after installation.

1 **GET SET UP.** Open the tub surround carton to check that all parts are there and undamaged. Then store panels at room temperature for at least six hours prior to installation. Gather the required tools, clear the room, and protect the floor and tub with drop cloths. Close the shut-off valves that control the water to the bathroom (see GET SET, p. 8).

2 **REMOVE THE HANDLES AND TRIM.** Pop off the decorative cap on the faucet to access and remove the screw that secures the handle (here, a single tub/shower unit). Pull off the handle and remove the escutcheon (trim). Remove the tub spout by loosening the  setscrew (a mirror helps you see it) and wiggling it off or by twisting if it's the threaded type. Unscrew the shower head arm, as well.

 **3** **PREPARE THE EXISTING SURFACE.** Remove any loose tiles, then clean the area to remove soap film, mold, and mildew. If there's a soap dish, use a mason's hammer and chisel to knock it off. Be sure to wear eye protection. If an adjacent tile is cracked in the process, remove it, too. Cut a piece of ⅜-in. plywood to fit the void so it is flush with no gaps, and adhere it with panel adhesive. With goggles and dust mask on, sand the tile surface with 60-grit sandpaper. A random orbit sander with dust collection, as shown in photo, does the best and quickest job. Remove the old caulk and wipe the area clean. Re-caulk to seal the joint between the tub and wall (see DO IT NOW at left).

4 **INSTALL THE TRIM.** For a neater edge, remove any existing edging, such as bullnose tile, and install wood trim (stop molding) painted to match the new surround. Cut it to fit from floor to ceiling and attach it to the wall with panel adhesive and 3d finish nails. Using a level, pencil a plumb line on the trim about ½ in. in from the outer edge. The end panel will be positioned flush against this line when it is installed in Step 7.

⊙ DO IT RIGHT

A template ensures accurate cut-outs for plumbing holes in the acrylic panel. Use packing cardboard, cut to panel size. Be sure the lower-left corner is perfectly square. Lay the cardboard aside and figure the locations of the cutouts by first measuring vertically from the centers of any pipes or valves to the tub. From that point, measure horizontally to the inside edge of the stop molding. Now, transfer the measurements for the plumbing cutouts onto the cardboard and cut the appropriately sized holes.

To cut large-diameter holes, such as for the tub/shower valve, first cut an access hole with a small-diameter hole saw.

✦ WHAT CAN GO WRONG

Write "FACE" on your cardboard template to ensure that you position it faceup when using it to guide your hole drilling and cutting. If you were to flop it accidentally the holes would be in the wrong positions.

Cut and Fit

5 **FIT AND CUT THE CORNERS.** Position each corner unit to verify that it contacts the tub squarely. If not, file the bottom edge with a medium-coarse file as needed (inset photo). Then position the corner units and check for level across the top using a level and

a straight board that can span the distance between the corners. If they aren't level, mark the amount that must be cut off the bottom of the corner units and then remove that amount with a file or jigsaw.

6 **ADHERE THE CORNERS.** Lean the first corner unit against a wall and apply the adhesive with a caulking gun as directed by the manufacturer. Then peel the paper backing off of the adhesive tape that, along with bracing (see Step 18), helps hold the panels to the walls while the adhesive cures. Rest the bottom edge of the unit against the tub. Carefully position it in the corner, and then press it firmly in place with outstretched fingers. Repeat for the second corner unit.

7 **CUT THE REAR AND END PANELS.** Test-fit each panel. The top of the rear panel should line up with the top edges of both corner pieces. The end panels should line up with the top of the corner pieces and the line you drew in Step 4. File or cut the bottom edge as needed. Then create a cardboard template for the plumbing holes in the front end panel (see DO IT RIGHT at left). Test the template for fit as shown.

8 **CUT THE PLUMBING HOLES.** Support the end panel faceup on 2x4s, with ⅜-in. plywood under the areas to be cut. Place the template (also faceup!) over the panel, align the square corners, and clamp it to the plywood. (The template both guides your cuts and pro-

tects the surface.) Use a hole saw to drill a hole for the spout and a starter hole for the tub/shower valve (see DO IT NOW at left). Use a jigsaw with a fine-tooth woodcutting blade for making a large-diameter tub/shower valve hole. Be sure to test-fit the panel after you cut it.

5

6

7

8

Use ³⁄₈-in. plywood to build out the wall above the existing tile to create a level surface for the extension kit panels. Secure with panel adhesive and drywall screws.

Prepare Extension Kit Pieces

9 **CUT THE EXTENSION CORNERS.** If your installation includes a kit that extends the surround to the ceiling, scribe the corners so they'll fit flush to the ceiling. Hold each corner in place, set the scribe to equal the overlap, and mark the corners as shown. Cut them at this line using a jig saw and test for fit.

10 **MAKE TEMPLATES.** To ensure that each extension kit panel fits perfectly against an out-of-level or wavy ceiling, cut and position a cardboard template that is 1 in. taller than the opening and about ½ in. narrower. (Use a straightedge and carpenter's square to make sure the template cuts are straight and that the sides are square to the bottom edge.) Adjust the template until the bottom edge is level and the top edge touches the ceiling at some point, then tape it in place. Set a scribe for the inch you need to remove from the template and use it, as shown, to mark the top edge for cutting. Also use the front-end template to mark where the hole needs to be cut for the shower head.

11 **CUT THE EXTENSION PANELS.** Place each template over its corresponding panel so it aligns at the bottom edge and is centered left-to-right; clamp the assembly to your work surface. Cut through the template and panel with a jigsaw that's fitted with a fine woodcutting blade. As you near the end of the cut, slow down and have a helper support the cutoff to avoid breaking the extension panel. If you need to taper a panel to fit against an out-of-level tub or ceiling, you can use a jigsaw and hand file. A belt sander with a 60- or 80-grit belt, however, will make the job go much faster.

12 **TEST-FIT THE EXTENSION PANELS.** As each panel is cut, position it atop the already installed surround corners. If it doesn't quite fit, file the top edge as needed to create a uniform gap (that will be caulked later). Then install the extension corners. Apply adhesive as directed to one extension corner panel at a time, peel off the adhesive tape backing, and press it firmly in place. Repeat with the second corner.

9 10
11 12

Install the Panels

13 **APPLY ADHESIVE.** With the corners and extension corners (if applicable) installed—and all panels test-fit—you are ready to install the rest of the panels. Lean each panel against a wall to apply adhesive with a caulking gun. This particular product has marked locations and specifies a ½-in.-thick glob of adhesive.

14 **INSTALL THE REAR PANEL.** Apply adhesive to the rear panel, peel off the adhesive tape backing, and position the panel carefully. Rest the bottom edge of the panel on the tub so it is centered on the wall. Then tilt it against the wall and press it firmly in place with  outstretched fingers. Verify that it aligns perfectly with the top edges of the corner pieces. If necessary, insert a shim (a small wedge) under the bottom edge.

15 **INSTALL THE END PANELS.** After a trial fit, apply adhesive and peel off the adhesive tape backing on one end panel. Press it into place, making sure that the outer edge is in line with the pencil line you made in Step 4, and that the top edge aligns with the top of the corner piece. Repeat with the other end panel.

16 **INSTALL THE EXTENSION PANELS.** If you are using an extension kit, install the rear and end extension panels next. Test-fit each one before applying adhesive and pressing it into place. As you did before, center the rear panel, and align the end panels with the penciled lines on the stop molding you drew in Step 4.

13 **14**

15 **16**

Complete the Installation

Before you caulk, carefully apply painter's masking tape to the edges of the surround and to the wall and tub surfaces where they contact the surround. Peel the tape off immediately after smoothing the caulk and drop into in a paper bag for disposal. Lightly smooth the caulk again with a wet finger.

Caulk the top and sides of the tub spout and faucet trim to prevent water from getting behind the fixtures and into the holes that you had to cut in the panel for the pipe and valve.

17 **INSTALL APRON STRIPS.** Scribe, cut, and file each apron strip for a tight fit against the sides and rounded upper corners of the tub. Support the workpiece on a thin piece of plywood and use a jigsaw with a fine-tooth blade to cut through both simultaneously. Use the rounded side of a half-round file to trim the curved section to fit (inset photo). Apply adhesive and press firmly into place. Then caulk the joint between the strip and the tub.

18 **BRACE OVERNIGHT.** Brace the wall overnight as shown, cutting crosspieces to fit snugly but without excessive pressure. Drywall screws may be needed here and there to secure the braces to each other. Take care to avoid screwing through the surround panels.

19 **CAULK.** After you remove the bracing, apply a bead of color-matched caulk along the top and bottom of the surround, and at vertical joints where the panels meet at corners (see DO IT NOW at left). If your installation includes an extension kit, caulk at the ceiling and between the upper and lower panels.

20 **REINSTALL PLUMBING TRIM.** Reverse the removal process to reinstall faucet hardware, trim, tub spout, and shower arm and head. Except for the valve, we ordered all new hardware so that everything would look up-to-date. Wrap Teflon tape clockwise around the threaded male end of the shower arm before turning it into the fitting in the wall and attaching the shower head. If your tub spout nipple is threaded, use Teflon tape on that too (see GET SET, p. 8).

17 **18**

19 **20**

Check out the accessories you can add to your tub and shower walls. They include bottle ledges and alcoves, grab bars, seats, and soap dish panels, such as these shown here.

Tub and shower wall kits are available in up-to-date colors and textures, including granite and tile look-alike patterns. They also come with a variety of shelf and seat configurations, so you're sure to find one that fits your lifestyle. Accessories such as bottle ledges and grab bars can also be added to make your shower surround as practical as it is beautiful.

Top-of-the-line tub walls are made from solid-surface panels. This modified acrylic, the same as used for many kitchen countertops, is very durable and resists fading. Trim kits for the outside of the surround are available in various styles and can include rosettes (inset).

This acrylic shower surround has a built-in shelf and seat and sliding glass doors. Tile was used on the border (inset) to give the installation a more substantial feel.

Tub walls can be trimmed with decay-resistant wood, such as cedar, for a more country look. These acrylic panels are molded to look like tile.

Photo Credits

All photos appearing in this book are by Carl Weese, except:

p. 27: (bottom) Photos courtesy of Quality Doors

p. 34: (bottom left) Photos by Charles Miller, © The Taunton Press, Inc.

p. 42: (left) Photos courtesy of American Standard Companies (Porcher line); (right) Photo © Mark Samu

p. 43: (left) © www.davidduncanlivingston.com; (bottom right) Photo courtesy of American Standard Companies

p. 45: © Brian Vanden Brink, photographer

p. 52: (top) Robert Perron; (bottom) courtesy of the American Olean Tile Company

p. 53: (left) Photo by Charles Miller, © The Taunton Press, Inc.

p. 55: © Susan Gilmore

p. 60: (top left) Doug Sandberg, courtesy of Tech Lighting LLC (2thousand degrees line™); (bottom left) courtesy of Tech Lighting LLC (Tiella™ line); (right) Thomas Lighting

p. 61: (top and bottom left) Robert Perron; (right) courtesy of Tech Lighting LLC (Tiella™ line)

p. 63: © Roger Turk/Northlight Photography Inc.

p. 68: (top left and right) Courtesy of LTL Home Products; (bottom) Robert Perron

p. 69: (bottom left) © Brian Vanden Brink, photographer; (bottom right) Photo by Scott Gibson, © The Taunton Press, Inc.

p. 85: (bottom) Photo © Mark Samu; (top left) Courtesy of American Olean Tile Company

p. 87: © Brian Vanden Brink, photographer

p. 92 (top left) © Brian Vanden Brink, photographer; (bottom left and right) Courtesy of Broan-NuTone LLC

p. 93: (right) Courtesy of Broan-NuTone LLC

p. 95: © Roger Turk/Northlight Photography, Inc.

p. 102: (top) © Brian Vanden Brink, photographer; (bottom) Courtesy of Stone House Building Products (CermaxxR vanity top)

p. 103: (bottom right) Courtesy of Kohler

p. 118: Photos courtesy of The Swan Corporation (Swanstone™ tub surrounds)

p. 119: (bottom right) Courtesy of The Swan Corporation

For more great weekend project ideas look for these and other
TAUNTON PRESS BOOKS wherever books are sold.

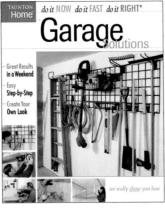

Kitchen Makeovers
ISBN 1-56158-726-5
Product #070797
$14.95 U.S.
$21.00 Canada

Garage Solutions
ISBN 1-56158-760-5
Product #070822
$14.95 U.S.
$21.00 Canada

Patios and Walkways
ISBN 1-56158-723-0
Product #070813
$14.95 U.S.
$21.00 Canada

Containers with Style
ISBN 1-56158-678-1
Product #070760
$14.95 U.S.
$21.00 Canada

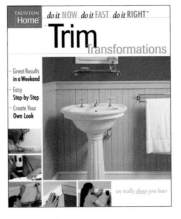

Paint Transformations
ISBN 1-56158-670-6
Product #070751
$14.95 U.S.
$21.00 Canada

Lighting Solutions
ISBN 1-56158-669-2
Product #070753
$14.95 U.S.
$21.00 Canada

Trim Transformations
ISBN 1-56158-671-4
Product #070752
$14.95 U.S.
$21.00 Canada

Storage Solutions
ISBN 1-56158-668-4
Product #070754
$14.95 U.S.
$21.00 Canada

For more information visit our Web site at www.doitnowfastright.com